James

PRACTICAL AND AUTHENTIC LIVING

BIBLE STUDY GUIDE

From the Bible-teaching ministry of

Charles R. Swindoll

INSIGHT FOR LIVING

Charles R. Swindoll is a graduate of Dallas Theological Seminary and has served in pastorates in Texas, Massachusetts, and California since 1963. He has served as senior pastor of the First Evangelical Free Church of Fullerton, California, since 1971. Chuck's radio program, "Insight for Living," began in 1979. In addition to his church and radio ministries, Chuck enjoys writing. He has authored numerous books and booklets on a variety of subjects.

Based on the outlines and transcripts of Chuck's sermons, the study guide text is co-authored by Lee Hough, a graduate of The University of Texas at Arlington and Dallas Theological Seminary. Most of the Living Insights are written by David Lien, a graduate of Westmont College and Dallas Theological Seminary.

Editor in Chief:	**Director, Communications Division:**
Cynthia Swindoll	Carla Meberg
Coauthor of Text:	**Project Manager:**
Lee Hough	Alene Cooper
Assistant Editor:	**Project Coordinator:**
Wendy Peterson	Marijean Armstrong
Senior Copy Editor:	**Print Production Manager:**
Marty Anderson	Deedee Snyder
Designer:	**Assistant Production Manager:**
Gary Lett	John Norton
Typographer:	**Printer:**
Bob Haskins	Frye and Smith

Portions of chapter five, "Plain Talk about Temptation," are from the study guide *You and Your Problems*, chapter 6, "The Problem of Temptation," coauthored by Lee Hough, from the Bible-teaching ministry of Charles R. Swindoll (Fullerton, Calif.: Insight for Living, 1989).

An effort has been made to locate sources and obtain permission where necessary for the quotations used in this book. In the event of any unintentional omission, a modification will gladly be incorporated in future printings.

ISBN 0-8499-8415-7

Printed in the United States of America.

COVER PAINTING: *The Angelus,* by J.F. Millet, from the Louvre, Paris—Scala/Art Resource, New York. The painting shows peasant farmers stopping their work to pray at the time of evening devotions or angelus, marked by the sound of bells from the church shown in the distance. Illustrations by Diana Vasquez.

CONTENTS

INTRODUCTION

Ever read about some person you wish you could sit down and talk to? Or, more often, haven't you come across the writings of a particular individual you'd love to spend an evening with? One of those people in my life is James. I am really drawn to this guy! He is practical. He is insightful. He is also gutsy, honest, and sincere to the core. He's a rare find today.

This study we are about to undertake will reveal just how true all these things are. You will find yourself thinking, "The man has been looking through my keyhole!" It is remarkable how penetrating and convicting the letter is . . . even though it was written about the middle of the first century.

Make me a promise, okay? Stay open and teachable. Don't resist the message of James, especially when he probes into the nerve center of your walk and your talk. He's right on target, pinpointing the very things that need our attention.

Someday we will be able to sit down and talk with James. When we do, it will be great to tell him how much we appreciated what he wrote, won't it?

Chuck Swindoll

Chuck Swindoll

PUTTING TRUTH
INTO ACTION

Knowledge apart from application falls short of God's desire for His children. He wants us to apply what we learn so that we will change and grow. This study guide was prepared with these goals in mind. As you go through the following pages, we hope your desire to discover biblical truth will grow as your understanding of God's Word increases, and that you will be encouraged to apply what you've learned.

To assist you in your study, we've included a section called Living Insights at the end of each lesson. These exercises will challenge you to study further and to think of specific ways to put your discoveries into action.

There are many ways to use this guide—in personal devotions, group studies, discussions with friends and family, and Sunday school classes. And, of course, it's an ideal study aid when you're listening to its corresponding "Insight for Living" radio series.

To benefit most from this study guide, we would encourage you to consider it a spiritual journal. That's why we've included space in the Living Insights for recording your thoughts and discoveries. We hope you'll return to those sections often for review and encouragement as you continue to grow in your walk with Christ.

Lee Hough
Coauthor of Text

David Lien
Author of Living Insights

James

PRACTICAL AND AUTHENTIC LIVING

Chapter 1

A CASE FOR PRACTICAL CHRISTIANITY

Survey of James

The Bible dwells on two prominent themes in its sixty-six books: the *way* to God and the *walk* with God. The first theme is directed to the lost, those dead in sin—it tells them how they can be saved. The second theme is aimed at the Christian, explaining how to live in a manner pleasing to God. Standing at the head of the class in this second category is the book of James.

When it comes to the subject of Christian living, James is one of the saltiest books of the New Testament. Its feisty emphasis on living out our faith is laced with practicality. You won't hear any mysterious, stained-glass theological discussions within the hallowed halls of this inspired letter, only grass-stained advice from someone following Christ in the grass roots of life.

Generally speaking, the book of James is not a great doctrinal treatise. The name of the Lord Jesus Christ appears only twice, and the author never mentions the Cross, the Resurrection, or the Holy Spirit. But this letter wasn't written for the purpose of establishing the doctrines of the faith. It isn't even a defense of the truth. It is simply a practical book that assumes you already know the basics of the faith; its intention is to drive home the importance of living out the truth.

In essence, the main issue that prompted James to write was this: If you say you believe, why do you act like you don't?

Before we begin our study of this book, let's acquaint ourselves with some important background information.

1

The Writer

The writer identifies himself as simply "James, a bond-servant of God and of the Lord Jesus Christ" (James 1:1). But which James? The New Testament mentions five men living in the first century who bore this same name. Most conservative New Testament scholars agree that this James was Jesus' half brother, born and raised in the same family.[1]

His History

For many centuries the erroneous idea has existed that Mary and Joseph had no other children besides Jesus. But according to Matthew 13:54–56a, there were several.

> And coming to His home town He began teaching them in their synagogue, so that they became astonished, and said, "Where did this man get this wisdom, and these miraculous powers? Is not this the carpenter's son? Is not His mother called Mary, and His brothers, James and Joseph and Simon and Judas? And His sisters, are they not all with us?"

If this list of names is given in order of birth, James grew up having to follow the sinless footsteps of his older brother Jesus. Growing up in the shadow of perfection couldn't have been easy. And things didn't get any better in adulthood, when this controversial older brother came home claiming to be the Messiah. How did James and other family members react? Mark 3:21 tells us.

> And when His own people heard of this, they went out to take custody of Him; for they were saying, "He has lost His senses."

The Living Bible says, "He's out of His mind." The Berkeley says, "He is deranged." Phillips' New Testament says, "He must be

---

1. "There was the James who was the father of the member of the Twelve called Judas, not Iscariot (*Luke* 6:16) . . . There is James, the son of Alphaeus, who was a member of the Twelve (*Matthew* 10:3; *Mark* 3:18; *Luke* 6:15; *Acts* 1:13). . . . There is the James who is called *James the Little* (*James the Less* is an error in translation), who is mentioned in *Mark* 15:40. . . . There is James, the brother of John, and the son of Zebedee, a member of the Twelve (*Matthew* 10:2; *Mark* 3:17; *Luke* 6:14; *Acts* 1:13). . . . Finally, there is James, who is called the brother of Jesus. Although the first definite connection of James with this letter does not emerge until Origen in the first half of the third century, it is to him that the letter has always been traditionally ascribed." William Barclay, *The Letters of James and Peter*, 2d ed., The Daily Study Bible series (Philadelphia, Pa.: Westminster Press, 1960), pp. 9–10.

mad." The decided opinion of the family, apparently including James, was, "He's a nut!" John 7:5 says, "For not even His brothers were believing in Him."

As far as we know, James' unbelief persisted even up to the time of Jesus' death on the cross. But 1 Corinthians 15:1–7 tells us that, afterward, the resurrected Lord Jesus visited James; and from that moment on, James appears in the Scriptures as a different man. In fact, he became one of the early church's most significant leaders, serving the Lord until he was martyred by stoning in the year 62 A.D.[2]

His Self-Perspective

It is interesting to note that in the introduction to his book— which, by the way, was the first piece of biblical literature written in the New Testament era—James does not identify himself by saying "I am Jesus' brother." That would have been name-dropping, something James condemns later in his letter as being a phony and empty practice. Instead, he simply identifies himself as "a bond-servant of God and of the Lord Jesus Christ." He recognized that his real relationship to Jesus was not physical but spiritual, made possible by the grace of God alone.

His Relationship to His Readers

In James 1:2, as well as throughout the letter, James identifies his readers as being "brethren." He uses this word in a way that means more than just "my fellow Jews"; this was a term specially designed for the Jewish believer of the New Testament.

James also refers to these people as being "dispersed abroad" (v. 1), meaning "scattered throughout," as one might scatter seed. There's a reason for this. The date was about 45 A.D. and Claudius was emperor in Rome. Under his rule the Jews had been persecuted and driven out of Rome and their homeland, Palestine. Jewish businesses were boycotted, Jewish children were mocked and thrown out of schools. Life was grim, threatening, and unsafe.

Someone has said that persecution purifies, but constant suffering crushes. And that's exactly what was happening to many of those early Christian Jews. They were buckling under the pressure of constant persecution. With their words they professed to believe; but with their actions they denied ever having known the Savior.

2. According to Flavius Josephus, as cited by J. Ronald Blue, "James," in The Bible Knowledge Commentary, NT ed., ed. John F. Walvoord and Roy B. Zuck (Wheaton, Ill.: SP Publications, Victor Books, 1983), p. 816.

Into this milieu of suffering and defection, James scattered a seed of his own—a powerful letter of exhortation and encouragement. Not about doctrines and precepts, but about maintaining a faithful practice of the Christian faith.

The Book as a Whole

Now let's turn our attention from the author to the book itself. We'll glimpse its unique features and get a brief overview of its contents.

The Main Theme

The heart of James' message can be summed up in these words: Real faith produces genuine works. If you say you've come to know the Lord Jesus, then that should be reflected by your life.

The Main Section

The primary section of this book is 2:14–20. The book's major thrust is contained in the first verse of this passage.

> What use is it, my brethren, if a man says he has faith, but he has no works? Can that faith save him? (v. 14)

Anyone can claim to be a Christian. But James points out that a person who has genuinely found faith will also walk in it. And he illustrates this principle with a down-to-earth example.

> If a brother or sister is without clothing and in need of daily food, and one of you says to them, "Go in peace, be warmed and be filled," and yet you do not give them what is necessary for their body, what use is that? (vv. 15–16)

James is not advocating a salvation by works, as some have accused him. Rather, he's advocating a salvation *accompanied* by works. Faith is the root; works are the fruit. Without fruit, words of faith are empty and lifeless. "Even so faith, if it has no works, is dead, being by itself. . . . Are you willing to recognize, you foolish fellow, that faith without works is useless?" (vv. 17, 20).

An Overview

The following outline of the book's four sections, together with the chart at the end of the lesson, give us an idea of the progression of James.

James 1. In this first section James asserts that when real faith is stretched, it doesn't break. Rather, it produces genuine stability. To prove his point, James uses three examples. In verses 2–12 he shows us that life's trials cause real faith to emerge. In verses 13–16 he says that lust's temptations cause a work of resistance. And in verses 17–27 he explains that when the true believer is faced with Scripture, the response is to change according to what it teaches.

James 2. The consistent theme throughout this section is that when real faith is pressed, it doesn't fail. Instead, it shows genuine love. Prejudice (vv. 1–13), indifference (vv. 14–20), and dry intellectual belief (vv. 21–26)—all these things are fought by real faith.

James 3–4. Here James affirms that when genuine faith is expressed, it is with control and humility, not unbridled arrogance. He goes on to say that we express our faith in three different ways: verbally (3:1–12), emotionally (3:13–4:12), and volitionally (4:13–17).

James 5. The final emphasis of this practicum on Christian living is that when real faith is distressed, it doesn't panic. Instead, it produces patience. James illustrates this message with everyday situations: not having enough money (vv. 1–12), sickness (vv. 13–18), and dealing with a brother or sister who isn't walking with the Lord (vv. 19–20).

Our Relationship to His Message

Those first-century Christians were struggling, and they needed some straight talk from someone who could help them cope. Today many of us need that same help—those of us whose vocabularies are bulging with all the right words, but whose lifestyles are shriveled for lack of spiritual substance. Martin Luther called the book of James a "right strawy epistle."[3] But as one commentator notes,

> It is only "strawy" to the degree it is "sticky." There are enough needles in this haystack to prick the conscience of every dull, defeated, and degenerated Christian in the world. Here is a "right stirring epistle" designed to exhort and encourage, to challenge and convict, to rebuke and revive, to describe practical holiness and drive believers toward the goal of a faith that works. James is severely ethical and refreshingly practical.[4]

3. As quoted by Blue, "James," p. 815.
4. Blue, "James," p. 815.

James at a Glance

Main Theme: Real faith produces genuine works.

Key Section: 2:14–20, "Faith, if it has no works, is dead . . ."

Key Terms: *Faith, Works, Doers, Brethren*

FAITH	WORKS		CHAPTER SECTIONS
When STRETCHED, faith doesn't break;	it produces genuine STABILITY.	C H A P T E R 1	1. Greeting (v. 1) 2. Trials of Life (vv. 2–12) 3. Temptations to Sin (vv. 13–18) 4. Response to Scripture (vv. 19–27)
When PRESSED, faith doesn't fail;	it produces genuine LOVE.	C H A P T E R 2	1. Partiality and Prejudice (vv. 1–13) 2. Indifference and Intellectualism (vv. 14–20) 3. Obedience and Action (vv. 21–26)
When EXPRESSED, faith doesn't explode;	it produces genuine CONTROL and HUMILITY.	C H A P T E R S 3,4	1. Expressions of Words—The Tongue (3:1–12) 2. Expressions of Attitudes—The Heart (3:13–4:12) 3. Expressions of Desires—The Will (4:13–17)
When DISTRESSED, faith doesn't panic;	it produces genuine PATIENCE.	C H A P T E R 5	1. Money Matters (vv. 1–12) 2. Sickness and Sin (vv. 13–18) 3. Carnality and Correction (vv. 19–20)

The ABCs of James

Author: James, the half brother of Jesus. See Matthew 13:55, John 7:5, 1 Corinthians 15:7, Galatians 1:19.

Background: The difficult circumstances of the scattered saints of that day caused many to drift spiritually. This led to unwise and unbridled speech, wrong attitudes toward God and fellow Christians, strife, gross carnality, and unproductive faith.

Characteristics: James has been called "the Proverbs of the New Testament." The book contains many practical, straightforward exhortations and great emphasis upon the importance of balancing right belief with right behavior. It includes many Old Testament references and word pictures.

Destination: Christians "dispersed abroad" in the first century. (James 1:1).

Era: Between A.D. 45 and 50. James is the earliest of the New Testament books.

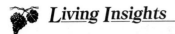 **_Living Insights_**

One goal of any study of Scripture is to seek out the author's intended meaning. One of the best ways to prepare ourselves to understand James' words is to read through his letter more than once. Find some uninterrupted time to read this entire short epistle two or three times. Saturate yourself with its contents, using a variety of Bible versions. It will be a tremendous help in leading you closer to the heartbeat of what James was saying to his first-century readers—and to what God wants to say to you today.

 Living Insights STUDY TWO

Before we begin digging into James' salt mine of Christian character traits, let's examine how well-seasoned our own lives are.

William Barclay points out that there were three special qualities associated with salt in Jesus' day. First, its whiteness was associated with purity. Likewise, the Christian is to be an example of purity. Second, it was used as a preservative to keep food from going bad. In the same way, the Christian's influence should protect against moral corruption. Third, the most obvious quality of salt was that it lent flavor to bland foods—the way Christians are to add spice to a spiritually bland world.[5]

- In light of these three qualities, how salty are you?

  _____

- How do you think someone like James, with his insistence on practical Christianity, would be received today in your church? In most churches?

  _____

  _____

- What is your initial impression about the relevance of this letter for you? What makes it so?

  _____

  _____

---

5. William Barclay, _The Gospel of Matthew_, vol. 1 (chapters 1 to 10), 2d ed., The Daily Study Bible series (Philadelphia, Pa.: Westminster Press), pp. 115–16.

Chapter 2

MARKS OF A PRACTICAL CHRISTIAN

Psalm 15

In our previous lesson, we saw that the intense and often brutal persecution the early church had to endure was creating a serious problem. Fear of suffering had caused many to retreat to a faith that existed only in words, not in deeds. Real Christianity was vanishing, either from Christians being hunted down and killed or scared into silence. Then God used James to write a letter focusing on authentic Christianity. A letter designed to prod real faith out of hiding. A letter that even today champions the cause for the preservation of the practical Christian.

In this lesson we want to get more specific about the marks of a genuine Christian. We'll do that by answering the question, What does a practical Christian look like?

Down through the centuries, many religious groups and denominations have attempted to define the image of a practical Christian with different lists of dos and don'ts, taboos, bans, and prohibitions. With such a variety of conflicting information, how can we know which list to go by? James' letter models a complete wardrobe for Christian behavior, but David wrote a psalm that provides the basic style. It's not about hemlines or necklines. Psalm 15 is a concise compendium of the practical characteristics that should adorn our lives as believers. It reads like a dress code of Christian behavior, one that we should all be able to agree upon.

David's Query

David opens Psalm 15 with two questions that ask basically the same thing.

> O Lord, who may abide in Thy tent?
> Who may dwell on Thy holy hill? (v. 1)

Here the words *tent* and *holy hill* are not to be taken literally but symbolically. Both are Hebrew idioms referring to the place of

8

God's presence, of spiritual intimacy.[1] In a poetic way, the psalmist is asking: What kind of person dwells in God's holy presence? Who can maintain intimate fellowship with the Lord? In essence, What does a godly person look like?

Two Parts to the Christian Life

In answer to these questions, David paints a beautiful portrait of a practicing believer from a palette of eleven rich traits. But before we step into David's studio for a closer look, it would be helpful to understand something about the realm of truth that forms the background for today's study.

When we acknowledge Jesus Christ as our Savior, several things become true in our lives—some related to our eternal inheritance and some related to our temporal experience.

Eternal Inheritance

Once we are *in Christ,* many new adjectives apply to our lives, whether we're aware of them or not. Adjectives like forgiven, justified, accepted, regenerated, free, adopted, reconciled, secure . . . the list is almost endless.

In addition, this new inheritance carries with it some important characteristics. *First,* it is given at salvation for all time and eternity. *Second,* it never changes; those adjectives will always apply. *Third,* the truths of the inheritance are not necessarily experienced emotionally. *Fourth,* this inheritance is established by God alone; it requires no amount of work on our part. And *fifth,* it is visible only to God, not to us.

Temporal Experience

At the moment of salvation, our temporal experience of Christianity also begins, with *Christ in us,* dwelling in our hearts through the Holy Spirit. As we give Christ control over our lives, we begin to experience power in prayer, the fruits of the Spirit, hunger for the Word of God, true worship, obedience to God, spiritual growth, witnessing, and practical insight.

Like our eternal inheritance, our temporal experience also has five important characteristics. *First,* each of these experiences relate to our earthly walk and determine the depth of our fellowship with

---

1. Psalm 91 begins in a similar fashion.

God. *Second*, these things develop and grow as we mature. *Third*, although sin has no effect on our eternal inheritance, it can hinder the development of His image in us in our temporal experience. *Fourth*, growth in each area of our temporal experience will come only as we depend on the Holy Spirit. And *fifth*, all characteristics in this realm are visible to both God and to us.

David's Answer

It is important to keep the differences between our eternal inheritance and our temporal experience firmly in mind as we work through Psalm 15, as well as the book of James. Both David and James are addressing issues related to the temporal experience of our spiritual life, not to our eternal inheritance.

Now let's peek over David's shoulder to watch and learn as he creates a composite picture of a godly person.

> He who walks with integrity, and works
>   righteousness,
> And speaks truth in his heart.
> He does not slander with his tongue,
> Nor does evil to his neighbor,
> Nor takes up a reproach against his friend;
> In whose eyes a reprobate is despised,
> But who honors those who fear the Lord;
> He swears to his own hurt, and does not change;
> He does not put out his money at interest,
> Nor does he take a bribe against the innocent.
> He who does these things will never be shaken.
> (vv. 2–5)

They Walk with Integrity (v. 2)

The Hebrew term translated *integrity* means "complete, innocent, or morally whole." Those who enjoy intimate fellowship with God have no hidden areas of shame in their lives. Their "walk," or way of life, is in harmony with God's standards. And, as Proverbs 20:7 says,

> A righteous man who walks in his integrity—
> How blessed are his sons after him.

One of the by-products of integrity is a happy family life. The guilty parent who lives under the constant fear of being found out injects the whole family with a mood of mistrust and unhappiness. But for those whose blamelessness enables them to live transparently before others, their homes will be swathed with warm, caring relationships.

They Work Righteousness (v. 2)

According to the *New Dictionary of Theology*, the term *righteousness* "denotes not so much the abstract idea of justice or virtue, as right standing and consequent right behaviour, within a community."[2] Those who dwell in the Lord's presence have made a habit of being ethical, honest, and straightforward in their daily conduct.

They Speak Truth in Their Hearts (v. 2)

Nowhere else in the Scriptures do we find this particular phrase, "speaks truth in his heart." Normally, we think of speaking as something done with our mouths, not our hearts. But in reality, it is the heart, not the mouth, that dictates what we say—"For as [a man] thinks within himself, so he is" (Prov. 23:7). Jesus commented on this distinction as well.

> "For from within, out of the heart of men, proceed the evil thoughts, fornications, thefts, murders, adulteries, deeds of coveting and wickedness, as well as deceit, sensuality, envy, slander, pride and foolishness. All these evil things proceed from within and defile the man." (Mark 7:21–23)

If we want to dwell in the Lord's presence, there must not be a credibility gap between our heart and our tongue. We must seek to speak the truth, the whole truth, and nothing but the truth. Always.

They Do Not Slander (v. 3)

The word *slander* is an interesting term in Hebrew. It means "foot or hoof of a horse," and it carries the idea of walking into a situation, looking it over, backing out carefully, and then hoofing it—going from place to place revealing secrets that are really no one else's business. Webster defines slander as "the utterance of false charges or misrepresentations which defame and damage another's

---

2. Sinclair B. Ferguson and David F. Wright, eds., *New Dictionary of Theology* (Downers Grove, Ill.: InterVarsity Press, 1988), p. 591.

reputation."[3] Slander, then, is not simply telling a lie; it is distorting the truth about another person. To avoid this, we must choose our words so carefully that if the people we're talking about were present, they would say, "That's exactly right. Those are the facts."

They Do No Evil to Their Neighbors (v. 3)

Literally, the word *do* or *does* means "to endure." The Living Bible captures the thought well: They do "not listen to gossip."[4] Believers not only avoid speaking slander; they don't endure, or listen to, slander either. One way to avoid being caught in a slanderous conversation is to simply leave. Don't hang around and, by doing so, lend support to what's being said.

They Do Not Take Up a Reproach against Their Friends (v. 3)

Here David uses the word *reproach*, meaning "something sharp or cutting." And he changes the focus from neighbor to friend, drawing the application of this trait down into our close relationships. After all, the cuts inflicted by friends go deeper because we have made ourselves vulnerable by opening up our lives and exposing our frailties.

They Despise a Reprobate (v. 4)

The word *reprobate* means "a worthless person." It is a strong term reserved for an avowed unbeliever who despises the things of God. The individual who draws near to God will find it impossible to have an intimate relationship with those who despise all that Christians love.

They Honor Those Who Fear the Lord (v. 4)

Romans 13:7 says,

> Render to all what is due them: tax to whom tax is due; custom to whom custom; fear to whom fear; honor to whom honor.

One of the obvious marks of practical Christians is the respect, support, and appreciation given to those who fear God—regardless of background, position, or race.

---

3. *Webster's Ninth New Collegiate Dictionary,* see "slander."
4. For further study, see 1 Corinthians 5:9–11 and 2 Corinthians 6:14–18.

They Swear to Their Own Hurt and Do Not Change (v. 4)

Simply put, practicing Christians keep their promises. When they give their word to do something, they do it—no matter how difficult it may be. In the eyes of others, the credibility of our Christianity will always be dependent upon our personal reliability, whether it has to do with paying back a debt, doing a job, meeting someone at a certain time, or sticking with a venture.

They Do Not Loan Money at Interest to a Brother or a Close Friend (v. 5)

More colorfully, "he does not put the bite on them."[5] At one time or another, we've all smarted from teeth marks left by those who have chomped down on us financially. So we ought to know better than to unleash ravenous interest rates on loans to close friends! According to Jewish law (Lev. 25:35–37, Deut. 23:19–20), a Jew was not to charge interest on a loan to another Jew. Why? Because love should prompt one person to assist another, rather than the greed of making a profit off someone in need.

They Do Not Take a Bribe against an Innocent Person (v. 5)

A practicing believer cannot be bought, whether on a jury, in a business, or in matters of trust in relationships.

David's Promise

For the one who practices these traits, Psalm 15 closes with a word of promise: "He . . . will never be shaken" (v. 5). In the experience of intimacy with God, we can exchange our own frailties and weaknesses for His stability and strength.

An Illustration

The life of a believer, like the one described in Psalm 15, can be compared to a tree. The visible part of our lives, our outward walk, is like the trunk and branches of a tree. Underneath the surface lie the inward qualities that provide roots and stability for the things that are seen. That solid foundation is especially important in today's society, where moral wavering is not only detected but actively looked for.

---

5. Allen P. Ross, "Psalms," in *The Bible Knowledge Commentary*, ed. John F. Walvoord and Roy B. Zuck (Wheaton, Ill.: SP Publications, Victor Books, 1985), p. 803.

This kind of scrutinizing isn't just a twentieth-century phenomenon, however. It was practiced even in Daniel's day. According to Daniel 6, King Darius appointed 120 satraps, or governors, to oversee his kingdom, as well as three commissioners to supervise his governors. Daniel was one of these three. Everything was fine until Daniel's work began to outshine the others'.

> Then this Daniel began distinguishing himself among the commissioners and satraps because he possessed an extraordinary spirit, and the king planned to appoint him over the entire kingdom. Then the commissioners and satraps began trying to find a ground of accusation against Daniel in regard to government affairs. (vv. 3–4a)

It sounds so familiar; scrutinizing the lives of public figures in high office has become a national pastime in our day. Unfortunately, there aren't many who come out of these close inspections with the same impeccable report as Daniel's.

> But they could find no ground of accusation or evidence of corruption, inasmuch as he was faithful, and no negligence or corruption was to be found in him. (v. 4b)

What kind of people can have their lives pinched, poked, and probed, as Daniel's was, and still be found blameless? Only those who abide in God's tent, who dwell on His holy hill through living the very real, the very practical life of faith described in Psalm 15.

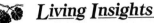 *Living Insights*

In this lesson we have used Psalm 15 to illustrate the truths we'll find in James. Now, can you illustrate and support the truths from Psalm 15 by using other Scriptures? In the following chart, write in some appropriate references from both the Old and the New Testaments.

Marks of a Practical Christian	
Character Traits	Cross References
Walks with integrity	
Works righteousness	
Speaks truth in his heart	
Does not slander	
Does not do evil to neighbor	
Does not take up reproach against friends	
Despises ungodliness	
Honors those who fear the Lord	
Swears to his own hurt	
Does not loan for interest	
Does not take a bribe	

 Living Insights

How well could you relate to the list of traits from Psalm 15? Can you think of practical ways you demonstrate these principles in your life?

Using that same chart from Study One, get a sheet of paper and record two or three very practical things you do that demonstrate each of these characteristics. If you find you are unable to write anything next to the traits, plan a little strategy to develop that area of your life.

Chapter 3

WHEN TROUBLES WON'T GO AWAY

James 1:2–12

Remember when you were little, how your arms and legs were always freckled with bruises? Like that purplish one with the yellow rings around it from the time you fell out of that tree you weren't supposed to be in. And how about the one that swelled up like a dark storm cloud when you rammed your shin into the oak coffee table playing got-you-last? Then there was the time you got the wind knocked out of you playing red-rover because Steve and Jerry's arms didn't give when you slammed into them. Afterward your whole chest seemed like one giant, throbbing bruise. Being a child meant having a body that was a constantly changing configuration of cuts, scrapes, and contusions.

But even as adults, we still make mistakes and "scrape our knees." We get the wind knocked out of us by unfaithful marriage partners, crippling accidents, or the sudden death of someone close. We may have traded climbing trees for climbing corporate ladders, but it still hurts when we fall. We don't cut our fingers much anymore, but we do hurt from cutting remarks that leave us bleeding on the inside. Nowadays it's our hearts, not our arms and legs, that are mottled with the black-and-blue marks of troubles. The day's cuts, burns, and spills leave behind painful emotional welts. We often feel as if we were, in Shakespeare's words, "a wretched soul, bruis'd with adversity."[1]

Adversity—it besets us all. A battered and melancholy Job sighed, "Man . . . is short-lived and full of turmoil" (Job 14:1). Even David, who enjoyed an enviable closeness with God, confessed, "Many are the afflictions of the righteous" (Ps. 34:19a). And Paul explained, "We are afflicted in every way, . . . perplexed, . . . persecuted, . . . struck down" (2 Cor. 4:8–9). Someone has said that if you were to trace Paul's journeys in the first century, it would be like tracking the path of a wounded deer running from a hunter, leaving one bloody trail after another.

---

1. Shakespeare, *The Comedy of Errors*, act 2, scene 1, line 34.

In our last lesson, we saw that James was addressing Jewish Christians who were literally bruised with adversity. They were being hunted under the persecution instigated by the Roman emperor Claudius. They had been hounded from their homes and homeland and were constantly being treated with hostility—by Gentiles, who hated them because they were Jewish, and by fellow Jews, who hated them for being Christians. These believers knew the bruised and bloodstained misery of troubles that wouldn't go away. James, therefore, in his letter, immediately went to work setting fractured and disjointed attitudes and binding bruised spirits with the Great Physician's truth about troubles.

What Is True about Troubles?

Today there are numerous ideas being tossed around regarding trials. Some people believe they're a form of punishment from God. Others dangle the promise before us that if we can just reach a certain level of maturity, trials will disappear and we'll live happily ever after; life will be one big spiritual Disneyland. And still others are out there trying to convince us that there's really no such thing as adversity. Trials such as death, pain, and sickness are a figment of our imagination; like the boogeyman, they don't exist.

James, however, has something quite different to say about trials.

They Are Inevitable

> Consider it all joy, my brethren, when you encounter various trials. (James 1:2)

Notice that James didn't say, "Consider it all joy *if* you encounter various trials." He said *when*. We needn't wonder if they'll come or when they'll leave. They're here to stay (compare 1 Peter 4:12). James also gives us fair warning about the kind of trials we can expect. The Greek word he uses for "various" is the one from which we get the term *polka dot*. By this he means that we can expect our lives to be spattered with trials of all sizes and shapes.

They Have Purpose

> Knowing that the testing of your faith produces endurance. And let endurance have its perfect result, that you may be perfect and complete, lacking in nothing. (James 1:3–4)

Trials do have a purpose. But before we can grasp what that purpose is, we've got to give up viewing troubles as simply bother-

17

some offenses and start seeing them as tests—tests specifically designed by God to stretch our faith, not simply our pocketbooks, friendships, or health. Rather than viewing them as our enemies, we should look upon these tests as servants that bring about the circumstances needed to help us grow.

God isn't interested in watching our faith get torpedoed by trials. What He does desire becomes clear when we understand the meaning of the word *testing* (v. 3). It comes from the Greek term *dokimos*, which means "approval." It's a word found on the undersides of many ancient pieces of pottery unearthed by archeologists in the Near East. This mark meant that the piece had gone through the furnace without cracking; it had been approved. God's desire is to help the clay vessels created in His image to mature in the furnace of trials without a crack.

In every trial, God's initial purpose is to produce *endurance*. This word comes from a combination of two words that, put together, literally mean "to abide under." God's "Good Faithkeeping Seal of Approval," *dokimos,* is applied only to those who persevere, or abide under, the tests He sends. Enduring those tests is what brings about the maturity that is God's ultimate purpose for our lives (v. 4).

How Can I Rise above Troubles?

Speaking from his experience as a prisoner in the Nazi concentration camps, psychiatrist Dr. Viktor Frankl said,

> Everything can be taken from a man but one thing:
> the last of the human freedoms—to choose one's
> attitude in any given set of circumstances, to choose
> one's own way.[2]

Trials can strip away everything but our attitude toward them. Let's briefly go back over the verses we've just covered and consider three key elements, elements that form the attitude God desires us to choose when we face a trial.

Consider It All Joy

The word *consider* (v. 2) in Hebrew literally means "to lead the way"; it's the idea of going ahead of something else. Here it is linked

2. Viktor E. Frankl, *Man's Search for Meaning,* revised and updated (Canton, N.Y.: Beacon Press, 1959; New York, N.Y.: Pocket Books, Washington Square Press, 1984), p. 86.

together with the attitude of joy. The Christian's mind-set, going into a trial, is to be positive.[3]

Knowing That the Testing . . . Produces Endurance

How can a believer be joyful, positive, and assured in the midst of a trial? Because we *know* (v. 3) that tests are designed by God for good, not evil. We know that they have a purpose and that we aren't simply "playthings of circumstance."[4] The heat of the furnace is not designed to make us crack, but to solidify and strengthen His character in us.

Let Endurance Have Its Perfect Result

The third key term, found in verse 4, is *let*, meaning "cooperate." Give in to the testing. Allow it to do its job in your life. Participate in the lessons the trial brings to teach you. James illustrates this enjoinder in verses 9–11.

> But let the brother of humble circumstances glory in his high position; and let the rich man glory in his humiliation, because like flowering grass he will pass away. For the sun rises with a scorching wind, and withers the grass; and its flower falls off, and the beauty of its appearance is destroyed; so too the rich man in the midst of his pursuits will fade away.

Both the brother who has nothing and the rich man with everything are enjoined to do the same thing: Let the test go on, regardless of your circumstances. Don't cut short the process that will bring about your maturity.

Why Do Troubles Overwhelm Us?

All of us know what it's like to flunk a trial. We remember the wrong responses—resistant attitudes, temper tantrums demanding instant relief—that have advanced nothing but our immaturity and

---

3. Let's be careful about what James is saying here. He's not advocating that Christians should deny the pain and sorrow they feel in the midst of a trial. "Indeed, [J.B.] Mayor points out that James does not say that trial *is* all joy; rather, he urges his readers to *count* it all joy, 'that is, look at it from the bright side, as capable of being turned to our highest good'." Curtis Vaughn, *James: A Study Guide* (Grand Rapids, Mich.: Zondervan Publishing House, 1969) p. 18.

4. Frankl, *Man's Search for Meaning*, p. 87.

misery. Why do we do these things? Why don't we hang in there? James offers two reasons why our troubles often get the best of us.

Lack of Wisdom

When tests come, especially the pop quizzes, we may not be prepared to handle them. But we needn't just sit there feeling doomed to failure. James says to pray for help.

> But if any of you lacks wisdom, let him ask of God, who gives to all men generously and without reproach, and it will be given to him. (v. 5)

The wisdom mentioned here is directly related to trials; it's not just wisdom in general. James is referring to the ability to view a test from God's perspective. Without this kind of wisdom, the ability to endure becomes elusive, and the goal of maturity may never be reached.

Lack of Faith

The second reason why trials overwhelm us is a lack of faith.

> But let him ask in faith without any doubting, for the one who doubts is like the surf of the sea driven and tossed by the wind. For let not that man expect that he will receive anything from the Lord, being a double-minded man, unstable in all his ways. (vv. 6–8)

James is not referring to saving faith, nor to a general kind of trust. He's advocating a sustaining faith that involves complete abandonment to God and His purposes in our trials.

Verse 8 gives us a name for someone to whom wisdom just doesn't get through—that person's called "double-minded." A double-minded person is someone who wants his or her own will and God's at the same time. Someone who, down inside, still has reservations about being completely yielded to God.

What Is Promised to Those Who Handle Problems Correctly?

> Blessed is a man who perseveres under trial; for once he has been approved, he will receive the crown of life, which the Lord has promised to those who love Him. (v. 12)

The first promise is of happiness, as we learn from the term *blessed*, which means "genuinely happy." In the Old Testament the word *blessing* is always used in the plural, signifying being happy many times over. This kind of happiness is impossible if it's dependent on circumstances, but it's available in abundance if we depend on the Lord in all our circumstances.

The second promise is of "the crown of life." James isn't referring just to a future crown to be received once we're in heaven; he's referring to the crown of a rich and full life to be enjoyed here and now. Historian and theologian William Barclay draws out several of the implications hidden in James' reference to this crown of life.

> In the ancient world the crown (*stephanos*) had at least four great associations.
>
> (a) The crown of flowers was worn at times of joy . . . [it] was the sign of happy and of festive joy.
>
> (b) The crown was the mark of royalty. It was worn by kings and by those in authority. . . .
>
> (c) The crown of laurel leaves was the victor's crown in the games, the prize which the athlete coveted above all. . . .
>
> (d) The crown was the mark of honour and of dignity. . . .
>
> . . . The Christian has a *joy* that no other man can ever have. . . . The Christian has a *royalty* that other men have never realized, for, however humble his earthly circumstances, he is nothing less than the child of God. The Christian has a *victory* which others cannot win, for he meets life and all its demands in the conquering power of the presence and the company of Jesus Christ. . . . The Christian has a new *dignity*, for he is ever conscious that God thought him worth the life and death of Jesus Christ. No man can ever be worthless, if Christ died for him.[5]

A Concluding Thought

Perhaps the only bruise that never heals is the loss of hope—the loss of confidence that adversities are purposeful, not random,

5. William Barclay, *The Letters of James and Peter*, 2d ed., The Daily Study Bible series (Philadelphia, Pa.: Westminster Press, 1960), pp. 57–58.

meaningless cruelties. Nietzsche said, "He who has a *why* to live can bear with almost any *how*."[6] James has given us the why about our adversities . . . and now we can do more than just *bear* our trials; we can actually choose to *grow* through them!

 Living Insights

This lesson describes all of us in some measure. There's not a person who hasn't known some sort of heartache, sorrow, grief, or trouble in his or her life. So this is for you. Now, let's work on our ability to observe in the Scripture. Read through James 1:2–12 and look for the following:

- Name some positive qualities that have the potential of being produced by the testing process.

_____

_____

_____

_____

- Now, what are some potential problems that are discussed in this passage?

_____

_____

_____

_____

- Write out verse 12 in your own words, emphasizing the results of testing.

_____

_____

_____

_____

6. Friedrich Wilhem Nietzsche, as quoted by Frankl in *Man's Search for Meaning*, p. 12.

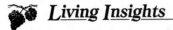 *Living Insights*

James 1:2–12 is a very comforting passage . . . especially to those experiencing some sort of affliction. Let's take the advice of the psalmist and "hide" some of the Word in our hearts.

- Let's dust off our memory skills and dig right into James 1, verse 2, and memorize through verse 4. Begin by reading each verse aloud, over and over again.

Chapter 4

HOW TO TRUST
WHEN YOU'RE TROUBLED
Job 1–2:10

When you opened your eyes this morning, did you look forward to the day, or could you barely force yourself out of bed?

If it was the latter, maybe you were just still tired. But maybe you're going through an overpowering trial that has drained your motivation and joy. Perhaps the pressures of that trial are even strangling your trust in the Lord—and now the long, graceful prayers that once flowed from your heart have trickled down to terse, sentence entreaties, disappearing into a brooding silence of unutterable anguish.

If this describes you, you're probably tired of people tossing platitudes at you like so much loose change: "Well, I'm sure it'll all work out," or "You'll make it; things will get better soon." You smile in response, but inside you feel that such glib phrases offer nothing more than a mirage of hope. They only salt your thirst for real comfort, and your heart cries out, "Lord, will things really work out? Am I going to make it? I want to believe so, badly, but I'm not sure I do anymore—and that scares me to death."

How do you trust God when a trial has swallowed you whole? What do you do when you're mired in muddling doubts?

Trusting God when we're troubled is not something we intuitively know how to do. We need a guide, someone who can lead us through the trial on a path of endurance and maturity. Fortunately, James recommends someone as an example for us to follow—Job (see James 5:10–11).

Many consider the book of Job to be *the* textbook on suffering. But in *Disappointment with God*, Philip Yancey suggests that the point of Job "is not suffering: . . . The point is faith: Where is Job when it hurts? How is he responding?"[1] And according to Job 1–2, his response is one we all should sit down and take notes on.

---

1. Philip Yancey, *Disappointment with God* (Grand Rapids, Mich.: Zondervan Publishing House, 1988), p. 165.

To find out exactly what that response was, let's follow Job through five dramatic scenes that switch back and forth between earth and heaven.

Five Scenes That Resulted in Calamity

The first scene takes place on earth; in it, we're given a description of Job's wealth and warm family life (Job 1:1–5). In scene two, the set shifts to heaven, and we're given a behind-the-scenes glimpse of who caused Job's troubles and why.

> Now there was a day when the sons of God came to present themselves before the Lord, and Satan also came among them. And the Lord said to Satan, "From where do you come?" Then Satan answered the Lord and said, "From roaming about on the earth and walking around on it." And the Lord said to Satan, "Have you considered My servant Job? For there is no one like him on the earth, a blameless and upright man, fearing God and turning away from evil." Then Satan answered the Lord, "Does Job fear God for nothing? Hast Thou not made a hedge about him and his house and all that he has, on every side? Thou hast blessed the work of his hands, and his possessions have increased in the land. But put forth Thy hand now and touch all that he has; he will surely curse Thee to Thy face." Then the Lord said to Satan, "Behold, all that he has is in your power, only do not put forth your hand on him." So Satan departed from the presence of the Lord. (vv. 6–12)

Job doesn't know about any of this—he's completely unaware that Satan has just wagered that he can make Job curse God. Yancey summarizes the situation with this helpful insight:

> Yes, there was an arm wrestling match, but not between Job and God. Rather, *Satan* and God were the chief combatants, although—most significantly —God had designated the man Job as his stand-in. The first and last chapters make clear that Job was unknowingly performing in a cosmic showdown before spectators in the unseen world.[2]

2. Yancey, *Disappointment with God*, p. 168.

25

With the background of Job's suffering understood, let's look at the third scene—Satan's attack on Job's faith.

> Now it happened on the day when his sons and his daughters were eating and drinking wine in their oldest brother's house, that a messenger came to Job and said, "The oxen were plowing and the donkeys feeding beside them, and the Sabeans attacked and took them. They also slew the servants with the edge of the sword, and I alone have escaped to tell you." While he was still speaking, another also came and said, "The fire of God fell from heaven and burned up the sheep and the servants and consumed them, and I alone have escaped to tell you." While he was still speaking, another also came and said, "The Chaldeans formed three bands and made a raid on the camels and took them and slew the servants with the edge of the sword; and I alone have escaped to tell you." While he was still speaking, another also came and said, "Your sons and your daughters were eating and drinking wine in their oldest brother's house, and behold, a great wind came from across the wilderness and struck the four corners of the house, and it fell on the young people and they died; and I alone have escaped to tell you." (vv. 13–19)

Talk about overwhelming trials! But before we look at Job's response to this carnage, let's shift to scene four, where Satan again presents himself before the Lord.

> And the Lord said to Satan, "Have you considered My servant Job? For there is no one like him on the earth, a blameless and upright man fearing God and turning away from evil. And he still holds fast his integrity, although you incited Me against him, to ruin him without cause." And Satan answered the Lord and said, "Skin for skin! Yes, all that a man has he will give for his life. However, put forth Thy hand, now, and touch his bone and his flesh; he will curse Thee to Thy face." So the Lord said to Satan, "Behold, he is in your power, only spare his life."

Then Satan went out from the presence of the
Lord, and smote Job with sore boils from the sole of
his foot to the crown of his head. (2:3-7)

While Job is still reeling from the previous blows, Satan strikes
him again—this time with a punch powerful enough to knock him
to the ground. But Satan suffered too, for he was humiliated before
all the host of heaven by Job's response to his blows.

Four Responses That Revealed Integrity

We've seen how this ball of pain got rolling, and we've seen
how Satan devastated Job's life. Now let's see how Job responded.

Worship

Job stood in stunned silence as Satan pummeled him with the
loss of his wealth and his family. But finally the catastrophic
punches ceased, and Satan stepped back to let his victim catch his
breath—and, hopefully, curse God. What Satan heard instead
struck a terrible blow to his pride that rang throughout heaven.

Then Job arose and tore his robe and shaved his
head, and he fell to the ground and worshiped. And
he said,

"Naked I came from my mother's womb,
And naked I shall return there.
The Lord gave and the Lord has taken
away.
Blessed be the name of the Lord."
(1:20-21)

Job's act of tearing his robe was an illustration of the tearing of
his heart; the shaving of his head was a customary rite of mourning.
And when he threw himself to the ground, it was in abject humility,
not to curse or ask why or to throw a temper tantrum, but to worship. His prostration wasn't a display of despair but a gesture of
adoration. Meredith Kline, a Bible scholar, says, "Behold, the wise
man! Not wise because he comprehended the mystery of his sufferings, but because, not comprehending, he feared God still."[3]

---

3. Quoted in *The Wycliffe Bible Commentary*, ed. Charles F. Pfeiffer and Everett F. Harrison
(Chicago, Ill.: Moody Press, 1962), p. 462.

27

In the Hebrew there is an ironic play on the words *curse* and *bless* in verses 11 and 21. Both words come from the same root word, *barak*, but they have two different meanings. Satan crowed in verse 11, "He will surely curse Thee to Thy face." And in verse 21 Job said, "Blessed be the name of the Lord." Satan used the word to promise blasphemy, but Job used it to deliver praise instead.

Humility

A second blow that must have sent Satan sprawling was Job's complete submission to God in spite of his losses.

> Through all this Job did not sin nor did he blame God. (v. 22)

Job's humility before the Lord came from the recognition that "God has the right to whatever He wants whenever He wants it. It is all His, because an owner has *rights*, and [we], as [stewards], have only *responsibilities*. . . . [We] literally possess much but own nothing."[4]

Silence

We can observe Job's next response as we see him sitting on a dunghill outside the city,[5] just after Satan has afflicted him with boils.

> And [Job] took a potsherd [a fragment of pottery] to scrape himself while he was sitting among the ashes. (2:8)

Instead of driving him to curse, Job's pain drives him to silence. To appreciate this reaction, let's briefly examine the severity of his illness. Job's whole body had erupted in virulent, itching, running ulcers. And these sores apparently brought with them insomnia, to say nothing of maggots and the sloughing off of dead skin (7:4–5). Some have even surmised that Job suffered from "elephantiasis, a disease so named from the swelling of the limbs and blackening of

---

4. Ron Blue, *Master Your Money* (Nashville, Tenn.: Thomas Nelson Publishers, 1986), p. 19.

5. The ashes referred to in Job 2:8 are a "mound of burnt dung lying outside the town. . . . There lies the outcast who, smitten by loathsome disease, is no longer admitted to the dwellings of men." Samuel Rolles Driver and George Buchanan Gray, *A Critical and Exegetical Commentary on the Book of Job*, The International Critical Commentary (Edinburgh, Scotland: T. and T. Clark, 1921), pp. 24–25.

the skin which disfigured the sufferer, so that his limbs and skin resemble those of an elephant"[6] (see 30:18, 30).

Job also suffered from terrifying nightmares.

"Then Thou dost frighten me with dreams
And terrify me by visions." (7:14)

For Job, each moment was swollen to its limit of excruciating, unending pain.

"And now my soul is poured out within me;
Days of affliction have seized me.
At night it pierces my bones within me,
And my gnawing pains take no rest." (30:16–17)

It's as violent and horrible a scene as anyone could imagine. But instead of bitterly complaining and shaking his fists at God, Job wraps his pain in a gauze of silence—a silence that his wife vehemently demands should be torn off and thrown away.

Then his wife said to him, "Do you still hold fast your integrity? Curse God and die!" (2:9)

Acceptance

In a fourth unforgettable response, Job reproaches his wife and goes a step beyond silence to willing acceptance.

But he said to her, "You speak as one of the foolish women speaks. Shall we indeed accept good from God and not accept adversity?" In all this Job did not sin with his lips. (2:10)

Three Reasons for Reinforced Stability

Before we close our study of Job, let's briefly look at three reasons Job was able to respond as he did.

First: *He looked up and was comforted by God's sovereignty* (see Job 1:21, 2:10). It would have been easy for Job to conclude from his circumstances that God was capricious and cruel. But instead of focusing on his circumstances, Job clung tenaciously to the comforting truth of God's sovereignty. He knew that even though he didn't understand *why* things were happening, he could still find rest in the understanding that God was in control.

6. Driver and Gray, *Commentary on the Book of Job*, p. 23.

Second: *He looked ahead and was reminded of God's promise* (see Job 19:25–27). By faith, Job looked ahead with assurance to the day he would rest safely in the presence of God, free from all the evil machinations of Satan.

Third: *He looked within and was shaped by God's instruction* (see Job 42:1–6). Under the excruciating pressures of his trial, Job eventually weakened. At the beginning, he sought God for an answer to the enigma of his circumstances. But this attitude gradually changed to a resistance of God's hand on his life. Job's questions became less a search for an answer than a demand of God to explain Himself in regard to Job's painful circumstances. But with the words, "I repent in dust and ashes," Job submitted himself as clay to the potter, to be molded by God without reservation.

A Final Thought

Someone once said, "We are all faced with a series of great opportunities, brilliantly disguised as unsolvable problems." According to Yancey,

> For Job, the battleground of faith involved lost possessions, lost family members, lost health. We may face a different struggle: a career failure, a floundering marriage, sexual orientation, a body that turns people off, not on. At such times the outer circumstances—the illness, the bank account, the run of bad luck—will seem the real struggle. We may beg God to change those circumstances. *If only I were beautiful or handsome, then everything would work out. If only I had more money—or at least a job—then I could easily believe God.*
>
> But the more important battle, as shown in Job, takes place inside us. Will we trust God? Job teaches that at the moment when faith is hardest and *least* likely, then faith is most needed. . . .
>
> . . . Every act of faith by every one of the people of God is like the tolling of a bell, and a faith like Job's reverberates throughout the universe.[7]

---

7. Yancey, *Disappointment with God*, pp. 172–74.

The next time you're faced with an unsolvable problem, let your trust in God reverberate with worship, humility, silence, and acceptance. If you do, you'll find that each of these will strengthen your endurance and deepen your maturity in Christ.

 ## _Living Insights_

If God were to allow Satan to move in on you as He allowed him to do with Job, how would you respond? Would God have a fight on His hands, or would He find you subduing the defensive responses of the flesh with worship, humility, silence, and acceptance?

• For the next few minutes, list three trials going on in your life right now, and write beside each one how you are responding to it. Is there a particular Job-like response that is missing?

Trial One

_____

_____

_____

_____

Trial Two

_____

_____

_____

_____

Trial Three

_____

_____

_____

_____

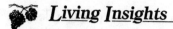 *Living Insights*

The book of Job is the journal of a man and his sufferings. It may be that you can relate to Job more than you thought you could.

- Why don't you take a few minutes to journalize not only the trials you are going through, but also how you are feeling about them. Use this as a time to lay your feelings before God.

_____

_____

_____

_____

_____

_____

_____

_____

_____

_____

_____

_____

_____

_____

_____

_____

_____

_____

Chapter 5

PLAIN TALK ABOUT TEMPTATION

James 1:13–18

Mark Antony was known as the silver-throated orator of Rome. He was also credited with being a brilliant man, a strong leader, and a courageous soldier—but the one thing he lacked was strength of character. On the outside he was powerful and impressive —but on the inside he was weak and vulnerable. This so enraged his tutor that on one occasion he shouted at him, "O Marcus! O colossal child . . . able to conquer the world but unable to resist a temptation."

That indictment fits not only Mark Antony but also many of us today. No one is immune to the bewitching appeals of temptation's sirens. And some, like Antony, find it virtually impossible to resist the pull of their alluring voices.

Countless people have wrecked their lives on the jagged reefs of immorality, drawn in by temptation's seductive song. Temptation, however, involves more than just sexual sin. We can be tempted by things and titles as much as by people. Students and businessmen alike are constantly being wooed to destruction by cheating's enticing entreaties. Many friendships lay battered and broken apart on the rocks where gossip sings. And floating face down beneath the choral urgings of power and popularity are the washed-out lives of leaders, pastors, teens, parents, executives, politicians—people who veered off course from following God for the tempting promise of fulfillment some other way.

According to Greek mythology, the crew on Odysseus' ship escaped the lure of the Sirens' beguiling voices by stopping their ears with wax. Unfortunately, resisting the kind of real-life temptation that Dietrich Bonhoeffer describes will take more than earplugs.

> In our members there is a slumbering inclination
> towards desire which is both sudden and fierce. With
> irresistible power desire seizes mastery over the flesh.
> All at once a secret, smouldering fire is kindled. The
> flesh burns and is in flames. It makes no difference

33

whether it is sexual desire, or ambition, or vanity, or desire for revenge, or love of fame and power, or greed for money. . . . Joy in God is in course of being extinguished in us and we seek all our joy in the creature.[1]

In our lesson today, James will be filling our ears, not with wax, but with important insights and truths about temptation—knowledge that will enable us to sail right on by temptation's beckonings.

Facts That Describe Temptation

Before we begin, let's establish what we mean by temptation. Webster defines *tempt* this way: "to entice to do wrong by promise of pleasure or gain."[2] Adding to this basic understanding, James presents us with four facts that we must all understand before we can even begin to deal with the problem.

Temptation Is Always Present in Life

Let no one say *when* he is tempted . . . (James 1:13a)

Notice the verse doesn't say "if" we are tempted, but "when." The moment we entered this world, we were drafted into a lifelong battle with temptation. The monk living behind the monastery wall is assaulted by it the same as the person who works in a busy downtown office. As Christian soldiers, we're not blamed for having to ward off temptations; none of us can eradicate the presence of these enticements. But we *are* responsible for our reactions to them.

Temptation Is Never Prompted by God

Let no one say when he is tempted, "I am being tempted by God"; for God cannot be tempted by evil, and He himself does not tempt anyone. (v. 13)

In his commentary on James, Curtis Vaughan points out that

man is naturally inclined to shift the blame from himself to God for his moral failures. One needs only to recall the words of Adam after he was charged with the first sin committed on earth: "And the man

---

1. Dietrich Bonhoeffer, *Creation and Fall* and *Temptation* (New York, N.Y.: Macmillan Publishing Co., 1959), p. 116.

2. *Webster's Ninth New Collegiate Dictionary*, see "tempt."

said, 'The woman *whom thou gavest to be with me,* she gave me of the tree, and I did eat'" (Genesis 3:12). In every age since, men have tried to cast the burden of guilt off of themselves and put the blame on God.[3]

In the Greek language, there are two different words used for our one word *by.* James' choice, in verse 13, strengthens his message that we are not "tempted by God." He could have used the preposition *hupo,* which would have indicated that God is not directly responsible for temptation. Instead, James uses *apo,* which shows that God is not even indirectly involved in tempting us to sin.

Temptation Follows a Consistent Process

> But each one is tempted when he is carried away and enticed by his own lust. Then when lust has conceived, it gives birth to sin; and when sin is accomplished, it brings forth death. (vv. 14–15)

These two verses form the crux of James' explanation of temptation. It is the only place in all the Bible where the process of allurement is clearly expounded. Here's how it happens.

First: *The bait is dropped.* We can be hooked by temptation like a fish by a worm because we're hungry . . . hungry for the fulfillment of our physical and spiritual needs. God promises to provide for these needs, but Satan also knows about our hungers. And although he cannot force us to eat, he is a skilled angler—knowing when, where, and how to drop bait in front of us that might lure us away from God.

Second: *Our inner desire is attracted to the bait.* The Greek word used for "enticed" is a fishing term. We all know that a hook baited with clothespins won't catch many fish! In order to pull that fish out from its comfortable hiding place, we've got to find a bait that will interest it, one that it can't resist. Once that bait is dropped and the fish sees it, it's as good as caught.

Bonhoeffer vividly describes what happens when our desire lunges for the bait.

> At this moment God is quite unreal to us, he loses all reality, and only desire for the creature is real; the only reality is the devil. Satan does not here fill

3. Curtis Vaughan, *James: A Study Guide* (Grand Rapids, Mich.: Zondervan Publishing House, 1969), pp. 29–30.

us with hatred of God, but with forgetfulness of God. . . . The lust thus aroused envelops the mind and will of man in deepest darkness. The powers of clear discrimination and of decision are taken from us.[4]

Third: *Sin occurs when we yield to temptation.* When we allow temptation to join the sinful desires within the womb of our minds, it gives birth to sin.

Fourth: *Sin results in death.* Even though sin sometimes brings a temporary period of pleasure, it always leads to death. James is not referring here to physical death, for then none of us would be alive. Nor is he referring to spiritual death, for then no one could be saved. The fulfillment of our lust brings about in the believer's life a death-like existence, like the one described by Max Lucado.

> Guilt creeps in on cat's paws and steals whatever joy might have flickered in our eyes. Confidence is replaced by doubt, and honesty is elbowed out by rationalization. Exit peace. Enter turmoil. Just as the pleasure of indulgence ceases, the hunger for relief begins.
>
> Our vision is shortsighted and our myopic life now has but one purpose—to find release for our guilt. Or as Paul questioned for all of us, "What a wretched man I am! Who will rescue me from this body of death?"[5]

Temptation Flourishes on Inconsistent Thinking

Do not be deceived, my beloved brethren. (v. 16)

Literally, the word *deceived* means "to be led down the wrong path." James issues this warning in the form of a command: "Don't allow lust to blur your thinking so that you forsake the truth to follow a lie." Surely there can be no more inconsistent thinking than to believe that giving in to temptation will lead to contentment.

Solomon tells us that the eyes of man are never satisfied (Proverbs 27:20). One more lustful look or one more piece of pie never satisfies. In fact, quite

---

4. Bonhoeffer, *Creation and Fall* and *Temptation*, pp. 116–17.

5. Max Lucado, *No Wonder They Call Him the Savior* (Portland, Oreg.: Multnomah Press, 1986), p. 139.

the opposite takes place. Every time we say yes to temptation, we make it harder to say no the next time.[6]

The battlefront for resisting being drawn away from God is in the mind. Each time we yield to temptation we believe a lie—and what's worse, we start living one too.

Focus That Determines Victory

James turns now from his in-depth look at temptation and focuses our attention on two ways for overcoming it.

Victory Comes through Dwelling on the Good

> Every good thing bestowed and every perfect gift is
> from above, coming down from the Father of lights,
> with whom there is no variation, or shifting shadow.
> (v. 17)

Someone once wrote, "Sow a thought, reap an act. Sow an act, reap a habit. Sow a habit, reap your character. Sow your character, reap your destiny." Victory comes from dwelling on those "good things" and "perfect gifts" that God has provided for us. The apostle Paul said, "Whatever is true, whatever is honorable, whatever is right, whatever is pure, whatever is lovely, whatever is of good repute, if there is any excellence and if anything worthy of praise, let your mind dwell on these things" (Phil. 4:8). If we sow these thoughts consistently, we should crowd out the weeds of temptation . . . and harvest more fruits of the Spirit.

Victory Comes through Living the Truth

> In the exercise of His will He brought us forth by
> the word of truth, so that we might be, as it were,
> the first fruits among His creatures. (James 1:18)

Every Christian has been brought to Christ through the "word of truth"—God's Word. And we are to continue to rely on His Word for deliverance in our daily struggle against temptation. In Psalm 119:9, David counsels, "How can a young man keep his way pure? By keeping it according to Thy word." And in verse 11 he says, "Thy word I have treasured in my heart, That I may not sin against Thee."

6. Jerry Bridges, *The Pursuit of Holiness* (Colorado Springs, Colo.: Navpress, 1978), p. 95.

Yet how many of us pray for deliverance from some temptation, only to turn right around and expose ourselves to it again? It has been said, "To pray against temptations, and yet to rush into occasions, is to thrust your fingers into the fire, and then pray they might not be burnt."[7] Christians cannot achieve victory over temptation with knowledge alone. We must sow God's Word into our daily living through obedience. Then temptation will begin to lose its foothold in our lives.

A Final Thought

Mark Antony's most widely known and costly temptation floated to him on a barge. Bedecked as dazzling bait, Cleopatra sailed up the Cydnus River straight into Mark Antony's unguarded heart. Their adulterous relationship, with its passing pleasures, cost him his wife, his place as a world leader, and ultimately his life.

Sow a thought . . . reap your destiny. Mark Antony wouldn't resist temptation. Will you?

 Living Insights STUDY ONE

As we enter the second section of James 1, we see that we're still talking about troubles. However, there are distinct differences between this section and the first. Let's see what they are. James 1:2–12 describes the process of *testing;* James 1:13–18 describes the process of *temptation.*

For further insights, use the following questions to compare Eve's temptation in the Garden of Eden to Jesus' temptation in the wilderness (Gen. 3:1–6 and Matt. 4:1–11).

• Are there any similarities in Satan's strategy between the two?

_____

_____

_____

_____

---

7. Thomas Secker, *The New Dictionary of Thoughts,* comp. Tryon Edwards, rev. and enl. by C. N. Catrevas, Jonathan Edwards, and Ralph Emerson Browns (Standard Book Co., 1966), p. 663.

- What was the first thing Satan attacked in the Garden? Why?

_____

_____

_____

_____

- Why was Jesus successful in overcoming the temptations thrown out by the Tempter and Eve wasn't?

_____

_____

_____

_____

- Can you think of any Scripture passages to back up your answer?

_____

Living Insights   STUDY TWO

No one is immune from temptation. So it would be a wise investment of our time to do a little self-evaluation.

- Temptation isn't limited to the sensual—our study has disclosed many other areas of lust. Very honestly, write down the areas of your life that are most susceptible to temptation.

_____

_____

_____

_____

_____

_____

_____

- Based on what you learned in this study, write out the temptation process that occurs in a particular area of your life. Include the outer bait, the inner desire, and how you yield. Be specific.

_____

_____

_____

_____

_____

_____

_____

_____

- Now, how can you develop the focus that determines victory? Look over the final portion of our lesson and see if you can develop your own game plan for victory.

_____

_____

_____

_____

_____

_____

_____

_____

_____

Chapter 6

HOW TO SAY NO
WHEN LUST SAYS YES

Genesis 39

It seems the older we get, the more we can appreciate the wit behind Oscar Wilde's words, "I can resist everything except temptation."[1] This Irishman's quip cuts to the heart of a dilemma that torments us all—one the apostle Paul had the courage and honesty to confess.

> It seems to be a fact of life that when I want to do what is right, I inevitably do what is wrong. I love to do God's will so far as my new nature is concerned; but there is something else deep within me, in my lower nature, that is at war with my mind and wins the fight and makes me a slave to the sin that is still within me. In my mind I want to be God's willing servant but instead I find myself still enslaved to sin. (Rom. 7:21–25 TLB)

Beneath Paul's frustration, and our own, lies the problem James spoke of.

> But each one is tempted when he is carried away and enticed by his own lust. Then when lust has conceived, it gives birth to sin; and when sin is accomplished, it brings forth death. (James 1:14–15)

Lust is not just desire, it's desire gone to seed—it's a bawdy, tempestuous, unquenchable craving for evil.

In *The Pursuit of Holiness*, Jerry Bridges states:

> Desire has come to be the strongest faculty of man's heart. The next time you face one of your typical temptations, watch for the struggle between your desires and your reason. If you give in to temptation,

---

1. *Bartlett's Familiar Quotations*, 15th ed., rev. and enl., ed. Emily Morison Beck (Boston, Mass.: Little, Brown and Co., 1980), p. 675.

it will be because desire has overcome reason in the struggle to influence your will. . . .

. . . If we are to win this battle for holiness, we must recognize that the basic problem lies within us. It is our own evil desires that lead us into temptation. We may think we merely respond to outward temptations that are presented to us. But the truth is, our evil desires are constantly searching out temptations to satisfy their insatiable lusts.[2]

Like Paul, we all get discouraged with doing evil when we meant to do good. We get frustrated trying to stop a Gulliver lust with a Lilliputian will. But how can we say no when lust begs, whines, and bullies us to say yes? Is it possible?

Today we're going to look at a memorable example of someone who found a way to say no to lust—Joseph. We'll find his story in Genesis 39.

The Historical Situation

Before we read about Joseph's temptation, let's look briefly at the circumstances that led up to the situation.

Joseph had ten older brothers, all of whom hated him. Their hatred was stirred by their father's favoritism and also by Joseph's unwise use of his ability to foresee the future. Finally, the brothers sold him as a slave to a caravan en route to Egypt, where he was bought by an Egyptian officer named Potiphar. In his commentary on Genesis, Henry Morris gives us some interesting information that will shed some light on our story to come.

Potiphar . . . was captain of Pharaoh's bodyguard, and also probably in charge of political executions ordered by Pharaoh. He is also called an "officer" of Pharaoh, the Hebrew word being *saris*, meaning "eunuch," or "chamberlain." It was evidently customary in ancient pagan countries, beginning with Sumeria, to require prominent officers associated closely with the king's court to be castrated, perhaps to ensure full-hearted devotion to the duties required of them and to minimize the possibility of

2. Jerry Bridges, *The Pursuit of Holiness* (Colorado Springs, Colo.: NavPress, 1978), p. 66.

their taking over the kingdom by military coup to establish a dynasty of their own.[3]

Here was a man of great wealth and reputation to whom Joseph was nothing but another piece of property. But

the Lord was with Joseph, so he became a successful man. And he was in the house of his master, the Egyptian. (Gen. 39:2)

God's blessing on Joseph's life, coupled with Joseph's personal integrity, led to his being promoted to a place of prominence. Eventually, Joseph gained Potiphar's complete and unreserved trust.

And it came about that from the time he made him overseer in his house, and over all that he owned, the Lord blessed the Egyptian's house on account of Joseph; thus the Lord's blessing was upon all that he owned, in the house and in the field. So he left everything he owned in Joseph's charge; and with him there he did not concern himself with anything except the food which he ate. (vv. 5–6a)

The writer of Genesis finishes this brief narrative of Joseph's professional life with a personal aside: "Now Joseph was handsome in form and appearance" (v. 6b).

The Sensual Temptation

While Mr. Potiphar is appreciating Joseph's reliable business sense and trustworthy nature, Mrs. Potiphar is becoming increasingly preoccupied with Joseph's good build and good looks.

And it came about after these events that his master's wife looked with desire at Joseph, and she said, "Lie with me." (v. 7)

Joseph immediately but politely refuses. He tries, first, to appeal to her reason and, second, to her conscience.

"Behold, with me here, my master does not concern himself with anything in the house, and he has put all that he owns in my charge. There is no one

3. Henry M. Morris, *The Genesis Record* (Grand Rapids, Mich.: Baker Book House, 1976), p. 559.

greater in this house than I, and he has withheld nothing from me except you, because you are his wife. How then could I do this great evil, and sin against God?" (vv. 8-9)

But Mrs. Potipher isn't moved a bit. She isn't interested in the sanctity of her marriage or the trust between her husband and Joseph. She's interested only in gratifying her physical lust—now. Nothing else. It's no wonder, then, that Joseph's spiritual concern also fell on a careless heart.

Peculiar Elements in Joseph's Temptation

Let's pause for just a moment to clarify some of the specifics in Joseph's situation. First, Joseph faced a difficult dilemma. The very place in which he lived and worked, Potiphar's household, brought him face-to-face with one very seductive temptation, Mrs. Potiphar. Second, the advances she was making surely must have flattered Joseph's ego and aroused his lust. Third, the source of temptation was persistent—she pursued him day after day (v. 10). Fourth, this woman pursued Joseph when they were alone, when there wouldn't be any fear of detection (v. 11).

It was a vulnerable time for Joseph. Undoubtedly, his lust was working overtime on his will, pressuring him to give in. "Nobody's gonna know. Her husband's gone, the servants aren't around, she's willing, so what's it going to hurt? It's done all the time."

The final test for Joseph came when Potiphar's wife resorted to more than just words to lure him to lie with her.

And she caught him by his garment, saying, "Lie with me!" And he left his garment in her hand and fled, and went outside. (v. 12)

Every time the issue of sexual lust is dealt with in the New Testament, we're told to flee, to get up and run. Some things we're to stand and resist. But when it comes to sensual lust, we're told to do exactly as Joseph did—get out of there. If we stay, we may just give in.

The Personal Ramifications

William Congreve once said, "Heaven has no rage like love to hatred turned, Nor hell a fury like a woman scorned."[4] All the lust

---

4. *Bartlett's Familiar Quotations*, p. 324.

that had burned in Potiphar's wife suddenly blazed into fury. She wanted revenge for her rejection.

> She left his garment beside her until his master came home. Then she spoke to him with these words, "The Hebrew slave, whom you brought to us, came in to me to make sport of me; and it happened as I raised my voice and screamed, that he left his garment beside me and fled outside."
>
> Now it came about when his master heard the words of his wife, which she spoke to him, saying, "This is what your slave did to me," that his anger burned. So Joseph's master took him and put him into the jail, the place where the king's prisoners were confined; and he was there in the jail. (vv. 16–20)

Joseph did the right thing. But once he got outside, he didn't hear any angels singing his praises for saying no. What he heard instead was the scream of a woman—a scream that would hurl him from the heights as Potiphar's overseer to the depths of an obscure jail cell.[5]

Practical Application for Today

Here are four important observations to help you in your struggle to say no when your lust says yes.

First: *You must not be weakened by your situation.* Several aspects of Joseph's position could have undercut his resolve to say no to lust. He enjoyed a secure, high-paying job with potential for advancement. His personality and accomplishments made him the object of praise. And, perhaps most dangerously, he had complete autonomy. He was accountable to no one. Those things combined make it easy to sin.

Second: *You must not be deceived by persuasion.* Mrs. Potiphar was bold, flattering, and calculating, and her proposition was tantalizing. No doubt her verbal enticements were as loosely clad and suggestive as she must have been. We'll never know exactly what

---

5. Even though Joseph was imprisoned as a common criminal, in the eyes of the Lord he was a very faithful servant, a model of 1 Peter 2:20: "For what credit is there if, when you sin and are harshly treated, you endure it with patience? But if when you do what is right and suffer for it you patiently endure it, this finds favor with God." And because of the Lord's blessing, Joseph found favor in the chief jailer's eyes. To see what happened next, read Genesis 39:21–23.

those persuasive words were, but here are a few we might hear today. "Your wife doesn't love you like she should." "By doing this, you will prove that you really love me." "Who will ever find out? We're perfectly safe." "Look, we're going to be married in a few months, so what does it matter?"

Third: *You must not be gentle with your emotions.* F. B. Meyer said, "Resist the first tiny rill of temptation, lest it widen a breach big enough to admit the ocean. Remember that no temptation can master you unless you admit it *within*."[6] As Christians, we must absolutely refuse to entertain lustful thoughts, even for a moment. Our resolve must be as firm as Joseph's.

Fourth: *You must not be confused by the immediate results.* Don't be surprised when your "Mrs. Potiphars" keep coming back to tempt you after you've said no. Saying no to temptation, whatever kind it may be, doesn't banish it forever. Lust doesn't give up that easily. Be prepared to have to say no again the next day, or even the next minute.

A Final Thought

Even with all these helpful insights, many of us are still going to give in to lust. And that's because of one basic problem. Jerry Bridges discovered this problem while studying 1 John, which

> was saying, in effect, "Make it your aim *not* to sin."
> As I thought about this, I realized that deep within
> my heart my real aim was not to sin *very much*. . . .
> Can you imagine a soldier going into battle with
> the aim of "not getting hit very much"? . . . We can
> be sure if that is our aim, we will be hit—not with
> bullets, but with temptation over and over again.[7]

Joseph had a commitment *not* to sin (Gen. 39:9–10). The battle of saying no to lust is really won or lost in our attitude toward sin. Before you go into the spiritual battlefield today, do two things. First, be sure to equip yourself with the helpful insights we gleaned from Joseph's story. And second, ask yourself, "Is my battle plan not to sin very much . . . or not to sin at all?"

6. F. B. Meyer, *Joseph: Beloved—Hated—Exalted,* new ed. (Fort Washington, Pa.: Christian Literature Crusade, 1955), p. 34.

7. Bridges, *The Pursuit of Holiness,* p. 96.

Living Insights

In his commentary on Genesis, Donald Barnhouse points out,

> Eve sinned by listening to the enemy long before she took the fruit. . . . Victory is won in the citadel of the mind far, far from the overt act of sin. Sin is so fascinating that it bewitches those who listen for even a moment. As a man cannot take fire into his bosom without being burnt (Proverbs 6:27), neither can he harbor sin in his heart without being corrupted. If Achan had turned from the bar of gold as soon as he felt a desire for it springing up in his heart; if David had turned away his eyes the instant he saw Bathsheba—how much shame and misery would have been avoided![8]

- List again your major areas of temptation, which you recorded in study two of our last lesson. Now examine whether your wall of resistance to each of these has been weakened. Are you committed to not sinning in these areas at all or to not sinning very much? If there are any breaches in your commitment, choose to repair them today.

_____

_____

_____

_____

_____

_____

_____

_____

_____

8. Donald Grey Barnhouse, *Genesis: A Devotional Exposition* (Grand Rapids, Mich.: Zondervan Publishing House, 1971), vol. 2, p. 170.

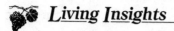

Living Insights

Looking back to the Living Insights in lesson 5, focus on that one particular area of your life where temptation is most likely to occur. Then take a few minutes to review the four practical applications from our lesson.

> If you want to say no when lust says yes . . .
> 1. you must not be weakened by your situation.
> 2. you must not be deceived by persuasion.
> 3. you must not be gentle with your emotions.
> 4. you must not be confused by the immediate results.

- How does each principle apply to your primary area of temptation? Jot down your thoughts. Use this as a time of therapy and cleansing before the Lord.

_____

_____

_____

_____

_____

_____

_____

_____

_____

_____

_____

Chapter 7

THE GREAT DIVORCE

James 1:19–27

Our topic today is divorce. Not the kind that occurs between a husband and wife, but the kind that occurs in a Christian between hearing the Word and doing it. The grounds for this type of divorce is not incompatibility but inconsistency. A. W. Tozer lamented,

> There is an evil which I have seen under the sun. . . . It is the glaring disparity between theology and practice among professing Christians.
>
> So wide is the gulf that separates theory from practice in the church that an inquiring stranger who chances upon both would scarcely dream that there was any relation between them. An intelligent observer of our human scene who heard the Sunday morning sermon and later watched the Sunday afternoon conduct of those who had heard it would conclude that he had been examining two distinct and contrary religions. . . .
>
> It appears that too many Christians want to enjoy the thrill of feeling right but are not willing to endure the inconveniences of being right. So the divorce between theory and practice becomes permanent in fact, though in word the union is declared to be eternal. Truth sits forsaken and grieves till her professed followers come home for a brief visit, but she sees them depart again when the bills become due.[1]

Thus far in our study, James has dealt with trials (1:1–12) and temptations (vv. 13–18). Now he comes to the basic theme behind his letter—the importance of behaving as we believe.

But before we begin a close inspection of verses 19–27, let's make four brief observations about the truth James presents. First, *it is imperative truth.* Verse 19 begins as though it were an indicative

---

1. A. W. Tozer, *The Root of the Righteous* (1955; Camp Hill, Pa.: Christian Publications, 1986), pp. 51–53.

statement, "This you know, my beloved brethren," but it ought to be taken as a command: "Know this." It's as if James is saying, "Listen up! This is important." Second, *it is family truth.* James addresses his readers as "my beloved brethren." Third, *it is personal truth,* "Let everyone." The truth is addressed to all believers in the Christian family. Fourth, *it is logical truth.* James carries his thoughts through a logical progression that involves (1) preparing ourselves for the truth, (2) actually taking in the truth, and (3) responding correctly to that truth in our daily lives.

Preparation for the Truth

Anyone who has ever painted a house knows that the hardest work is preparing the surface, not the actual painting. This is true in every endeavor, and for good reason. The better the preparation, the better and more lasting the results. As in painting, preparation is necessary also for receiving truth. Without preparation, we simply whitewash our lives with knowledge, which will quickly peel, revealing an unchanged character underneath.

James had seen too many Christians who tried to slap on God's truth without properly preparing themselves so that it would stick. So beginning in verse 19, he sets forth four requisites for preparing ourselves to receive God's truth.

An Open Ear

The first essential is an open ear.

> This you know, my beloved brethren. But let everyone be quick to hear. (v. 19a)

One reason our lives are often divorced from the truth is because we don't really hear what God says. The problem isn't that we're hard of hearing, it's that we're hard of *listening.* Jesus constantly rebuked the Pharisees for this very problem with the stinging question, "Have you not heard?" The obvious answer, of course, was yes, they had heard God's Word. The Pharisees were known for their meticulous knowledge of the Law. But they didn't really listen to what they read; they didn't allow God's truth to speak to them personally, individually.

A Controlled Tongue

Second, James says,

> Let everyone be . . . slow to speak. (v. 19)

A young man once approached Socrates to ask if the philosopher would teach him the gift of oratory. His request was then followed by an incessant stream of words until, finally, Socrates placed his hand over the inquirer's mouth and said, "Young man, I will have to charge you a double fee." When the fellow asked why, Socrates said, "I will have to teach you two sciences. First, how to hold your tongue, and then, how to use it."[2]

No one can speak and learn at the same time. How much time do you spend in silence preparing yourself for the sowing of God's Word? Before we can listen, we must first learn to control our tongues.

A Calm Spirit

Third, James says,

Let everyone be . . . slow to anger. (v. 19)

Why?

For the anger of man does not achieve the righteousness of God. (v. 20)

The seed of God's Word cannot take root in a heart overrun with resentment and revenge. We must tear out the tendrils of anger in our hearts before they strangle the truth that's trying to blossom in our lives.

A Clean Heart

The final step of preparation is a clean heart. To achieve that, James says we must do two things.

Therefore putting aside all filthiness and all that remains of wickedness. (v. 21a)

William Barclay explains that the word *filthiness* is a vivid term derived from the Greek word *rupos*,

and, when *rupos* is used in a medical sense, it means *wax in the ear.* It is just possible that it still retains that meaning here; and that James is telling his readers to get rid of everything which would stop their

2. Spiros Zodhiates, *The Behavior of Belief* (Grand Rapids, Mich.: William B. Eerdmans Publishing Co., 1959), p. 94.

ears to the true word of God. When wax gathers in the ear, it can make a man deaf; and a man's sins can make him deaf to God.[3]

In addition to ridding ourselves of obvious "filthiness," we're also to put aside "all that remains of wickedness." The Greek term for *wickedness* refers to hidden sins, motives, and attitudes that cause the corrupt outer behavior that others see.

Reception of the Truth

Now that James has shown us how to prepare ourselves for the truth, he next provides us with two important insights into the process of actually receiving truth.

In humility receive the word implanted, which is able to save your souls. (v. 21b)

One essential ingredient for receiving truth is having the right attitude. James wants our attitude to reflect humility, which means "with gentleness, openness; having a teachable spirit." Coupled with this, he says there must also be an action—"receive"—meaning "welcome." So, whenever truth knocks, we're to open the door and welcome it with great hospitality.

Response to the Truth

Many Christians end up with lives that are divorced from truth because they think that simply agreeing with Scripture is the same as obeying it. James, however, urges us to go beyond preparing and receiving; we must also act on what we've heard.

The Command

But prove yourselves doers of the word, and not merely hearers who delude themselves. (v. 22)

Notice James doesn't say *just* "be doers." God isn't looking for activists who don't know His Word. Nor is He interested in hearers who know His Word but do nothing. The Greek term for *hearers* is an interesting one. It refers to someone who audits a course at a

3. William Barclay, *The Letters of James and Peter*, rev. ed., The Daily Study Bible series (Philadelphia, Pa.: Westminster Press, 1976), p. 57.

university—someone who listens carefully and takes notes, but has no assignments, tests, or responsibilities. In short, someone who merely takes in information.

James plainly states that those who simply audit the faith are deceiving themselves about their Christianity, and that sincere believers will prove their authenticity by applying what they hear.

The Illustration

Immediately following his command in verse 22, James describes two different types of people, the hearer and the doer.

> For if anyone is a hearer of the word and not a doer, he is like a man who looks at his natural face in a mirror; for once he has looked at himself and gone away, he has immediately forgotten what kind of person he was. But one who looks intently at the perfect law, the law of liberty, and abides by it, not having become a forgetful hearer but an effectual doer, this man shall be blessed in what he does. (vv. 23–25)

In this classic metaphor, God's Word is compared to a mirror. But unlike a mirror, which only reflects outward appearance, the Scriptures reveal our inner character. The hearer James describes promptly forgets what both reflect; while the effectual doer, on the other hand, gives careful attention to the Scriptures, responds positively, applies what is heard and, thus, is genuinely fulfilled.

The Application

The effectual doer obeys what the Scriptures reveal and, in turn, becomes a mirror reflecting real Christianity. How can we know when someone is an effectual doer?

When there is no divorce between the truth and the tongue.

> If anyone thinks himself to be religious, and yet does not bridle his tongue but deceives his own heart, this man's religion is worthless. (v. 26)

When there is no divorce between the truth and the needs of others.

> This is pure and undefiled religion in the sight of our God and Father, to visit orphans and widows in their distress. (v. 27a)

When there is no divorce between the truth and our Christian uniqueness in a fallen world.

To keep oneself unstained by the world. (v. 27b)

Is your life on the rocks because you've allowed truth and practice to drift apart? Have your mind and will become estranged from one another? If so, it's time to start reconciling the two; you can by taking James' counsel to heart . . . *prepare, receive,* and *apply.*

Living Insights

Let's take a closer look now into the text of James 1:19–27 to see how prepared you are for the truth, how receptive you are of it, and how responsive you are to it.

Are you ☐ quick to hear? ☐ moderately quick to hear?
☐ moderately slow to hear? ☐ slow to hear?

Are you ☐ slow to speak? ☐ moderately slow to speak?
☐ moderately quick to speak? ☐ quick to speak?

Are you ☐ slow to anger? ☐ moderately slow to anger?
☐ moderately quick to anger? ☐ quick to anger?

Of those three qualities James urges us to emulate—quick to hear, slow to speak, slow to anger—which do you struggle with most?

_____

What are some things you could do to change that habit?

_____

_____

_____

Before the seed of the Word can grow in your life significantly, the soil needs to be prepared to receive it. Do some toxic chemicals in your heart need to be washed from that soil? Isolate any trace elements of filth or wickedness that are threatening your spiritual growth.

_____

_____

How humble is your heart? Any clods of personal or intellectual pride that need to be broken up before the Word can get really rooted in your life? If so, describe them.

_____

_____

What can you do to break up those clods?

_____

_____

Living Insights

Today's study focused on the disparity between what we believe and how we behave. Now it's time to hold up the mirror of the Word to see if that disparity exists in your life. In the column on the left, briefly write your beliefs about the following topics. On the right, jot down your behavior as it relates to each of those topics. We've done the first one for you as an example.

What You Believe	How You Behave
Jesus *is the Son of God and Lord not only of the universe but of my life.*	*My life reveals Jesus to be more of a part-time consultant than my full-time master*
Jesus _____	_____
The Bible _____	_____

55

Sin _____ _____

_____ _____

_____ _____

_____ _____

Prayer _____ _____

_____ _____

_____ _____

_____ _____

The Poor and Sick _____ _____

_____ _____

_____ _____

_____ _____

Loving Other Christians _____ _____

_____ _____

_____ _____

_____ _____

Loving Your Enemies _____ _____

_____ _____

_____ _____

_____ _____

Now step back a minute to glimpse a full-length reflection of yourself in the mirror of the Word. What do you see? A person whose beliefs and behavior are one? Or a person who presents a double image? If the latter, which is the *real* you? Is your life defined by what you believe biblically? Or does your behavior contradict what you claim to believe?

Chapter 8

PRESCRIPTION FOR MARRIAGE ON THE ROCKS
Psalm 51

Maybe you didn't hear any wedding bells, but did you know that when you trusted Christ as Savior He became your "husband" and you His "bride"? It's true. Once you tied the knot by faith you were immediately wed to Christ by "the Holy Spirit of promise, who is given as a pledge" (Eph. 1:13b–14a; see also 2 Cor. 11:2; Eph. 5:22–32).

The Old Testament also uses the marriage analogy, but often the focus is on a marriage that's on the rocks. Many times the words "played the harlot" or "unfaithful" are employed to characterize those who forsake God to worship pagan idols (see Judg. 8:27, 33; Josh. 22:16). This spiritual adultery, as we saw in our last lesson, can rupture into a divorce between the truth and the way a believer lives.

In today's lesson we want to look not at the causes of this split but at what we can do to restore our marriage with Christ when we feel it's crumbling.

Is it possible to mend this relationship—no matter how unfaithful we've been? Psalm 51 assures us that it is. Written by King David after a heated rebuke from the prophet Nathan, this psalm reflects the devastation of David's sin and also the gracious restoration that came after his repentance. Almost a year before he wrote this heartfelt hymn, David had committed adultery with Bathsheba, which resulted in murder, hypocrisy, and sorrow for the whole kingdom of Israel. God finally sent a no-nonsense prophet to the king who poignantly revealed how far he had drifted spiritually. For the rest of our lesson, let's listen to what David wrote in Psalm 51, a psalm which could appropriately be subtitled, "What to do when you've blown it."

Claim God's Grace

In Psalm 51, David's first response following Nathan's blast is to claim God's grace.

> Be gracious to me, O God, according to Thy
> lovingkindness;

According to the greatness of Thy compassion
blot out my transgressions. (v. 1)

David knows that he's guilty. He also knows that if God gaveled out justice, he would deserve to die on the spot. So the king reaches for his only hope of forgiveness, God's grace. What constitutes this grace? According to verse 1, it's a unique blend of God's loving-kindness and His great compassion.

One classic illustration of God's gracious forgiveness is found in Psalm 103:12.

As far as the east is from the west,
So far has He removed our transgressions from us.

Have you ever tried going west until you found east? It's impossible! No matter how far west you go, you can still go farther. The psalmist's point is simply this: When God forgives us, He places an infinite distance between us and our sin. People may tend to remind us of our past failures, but God completely removes them. This same truth is also depicted in Micah 7:19.

He will again have compassion on us;
He will tread our iniquities under foot.
Yes, Thou wilt cast all their sins
Into the depths of the sea.

God could keep all our shortcomings on permanent file in heaven. But instead He buries them at the bottom of the sea. That's grace.

Confess Your Sins

Assured of God's grace, David then proceeds to humbly confess his sins (Ps. 51:1–4). From his confession, we can learn three helpful specifics to apply in our own lives.

Address Them by Name

David is very candid about his sins. In verse 1 he calls them "my transgressions." In verse 2, David prays; "Wash me thoroughly from my iniquity, and cleanse me from my sin." He admits it as "my iniquity" and "my sin." In addition, he also portrays his sin with three pictures. In the first one, he portrays his sin as a crime, asking for pardon: "be gracious" (v. 1a). In the second, as a debt, asking God to "blot [them] out" (v. 1b). And in the third, as a stain, asking God to "wash him thoroughly" (v. 2).

Accept Full Responsibility

Notice also that David accepted full responsibility for his sin. He didn't come up with any elaborate rationalizations or attempts to shift the blame—"Lord, if it hadn't been for Bathsheba . . ." He simply admitted the hard truth.

> For I know my transgressions,
> And my sin is ever before me.
> Against Thee, Thee only, I have sinned,
> And done what is evil in Thy sight,
> So that Thou art justified when Thou dost speak,
> And blameless when Thou dost judge. (vv. 3–4)

Acknowledge the Cause and Effect

> Behold, I was brought forth in iniquity,
> And in sin my mother conceived me. (v. 5)

David isn't saying here that his mother was involved in a sinful act when he was conceived. Rather, he's saying that he received from his parents the same sinful nature all humans possess and pass on to their offspring. David is acknowledging that the basic cause behind every sin is a nature that is "prone to wander . . . prone to leave the God I love,"[1] as the hymnist wrote.

We can draw out another significant cause for David's sin from between the lines of verse 6:

> Behold, Thou dost desire truth in the innermost being,
> And in the hidden part Thou wilt make me know wisdom.

What's implied here is that, unlike God, David had not desired the truth. For a time he had chosen to ignore it and live according to his own sinful choices. What was the effect of forsaking the truth? We can see it in what he asks God to do in verse 8.

> Make me to hear joy and gladness,
> Let the bones which Thou hast broken rejoice.

While David was unrepentant, his emotional health ebbed, taking his joy with it. Most likely his unconfessed sin even took its toll on his physical health (see Ps. 32:3–4).

1. Robert Robinson, "Come, Thou Fount of Every Blessing," in *Hymns for the Family of God* (Nashville, Tenn.: Paragon Associates, 1976), no. 318.

Construct New Patterns

As we move into Psalm 51:10–12, David's thoughts shift from correction to construction—beginning new patterns of living.

Renew Me!

> Create in me a clean heart, O God,
> And renew a steadfast spirit within me. (v. 10)

David asks God to create in him a *clean* heart, one that's completely different from the sinful one he received from his parents. What happens to the old heart, the old lifestyle? When genuine confession is made, it is removed and buried; and in its place God gives us a clean, fresh start. Following confession, what did David need to nurture a clean heart? A steadfast spirit, meaning a disciplined mind that controls the emotions and guides the will to cleave to Christ and forsake sin.

Just as David reaches up for a clean heart and a steadfast spirit, two fears suddenly threaten to stop him, fears that haunt those who abandon the Lord for an extended period of time. The first is a fear that God will reject him, so David seeks reassurance.

> Do not cast me away from Thy presence. (v. 11a)

David's second fear is that God will withdraw His presence from him by taking away His Holy Spirit.

> And do not take Thy Holy Spirit from me.
> (v. 11b)

If we skip down to verses 16–17, we find that David's fears were relieved when he remembers God's merciful character.

> For Thou dost not delight in sacrifice, otherwise I
>   would give it;
> Thou art not pleased with burnt offering.
> The sacrifices of God are a broken spirit;
> A broken and a contrite heart, O God, Thou wilt
>   not despise.

David's broken and contrite heart found rest in the tender, forgiving arms of his God.

Restore Me!

Once his fears have been voiced, David then follows up his plea for renewal with a request for restoration.

Restore to me the joy of Thy salvation,
And sustain me with a willing spirit. (v. 12)

What needs to be restored? Joy and submission. David yearns for the joy he once knew, the joy which came from having a heart that willingly obeyed God.

Communicate Your Change

Once you have claimed God's grace, confessed your transgressions, and constructed new life patterns, then what do you do? David says we should share God's mercy with others.

Teach Sinners

Then I will teach transgressors Thy ways,
And sinners will be converted to Thee. (v. 13)

David knows the ways of transgressors because he has been one. He knows their heartaches and fears. And he also knows the Lord and how to bring the two together.

Praise God

Another way of communicating your change is by praising God.

Deliver me from bloodguiltiness, O God, Thou
God of my salvation;
Then my tongue will joyfully sing of Thy
righteousness.
O Lord, open my lips,
That my mouth may declare Thy praise.
(vv. 14–15)

For almost a year, this songwriter and musician had been silent. Now he's eager to dust off his instrument and loose the praises in his heart. But notice that David first seeks God's help in freeing him from the guilt of his past sins (v. 14a).

Is your obedience to God motivated by guilt or grace? When you've sinned, do you feel that you have to perform a long list of religious acts for God to accept you back? People may require us to jump through hoops to earn *their* acceptance, but God never does. He simply desires a heart that is humble, willing to be used again, eager to sing His praises once more.

Remember the Offended

In a very real sense, we all have our own kingdoms made up of family, friends, work associates, and myriads of other familiar faces.

And, like David, when we wander into regions of sin it offends others and brings them suffering. So David asks God for help concerning Israel, because he realizes that the whole kingdom has reeled under the weight of his sin.

> By Thy favor do good to Zion;
> Build the walls of Jerusalem.
> Then Thou wilt delight in righteous sacrifices,
> In burnt offering and whole burnt offering;
> Then young bulls will be offered on Thine altar.
> (vv. 18-19)

In Conclusion

Two leaves are pictured in the poem, "A New Leaf." One, a ruined page of school work; the other, a blemished page from a year of someone's life. Weaving them together, the poet presents us with a beautiful reminder of God's forgiveness and grace.

> He came to my desk with a quivering lip—
>   The lesson was done—
> "Dear teacher, I want a new leaf," he said;
>   "I have spoiled this one."
> In place of the leaf so stained and blotted,
> I gave him a new one all unspotted,
>   And into his sad eyes smiled—
> "Do better now, my child."
>
> I went to the throne with a quivering soul—
>   The old year was done—
> "Dear Father, hast Thou a new leaf for me?
>   I have spoiled this one."
> He took the old leaf, soiled and blotted,
> And gave me a new one all unspotted,
>   And into my sad heart smiled—
> "Do better now, my child."[2]

Are you hesitating to follow David in restoring your marriage with Christ? Are you afraid of rejection? that it's too late? that you've sinned too much? To Christ, it's never too late. No matter how unfaithful the bride, she will always find the bridegroom eager to cleanse her from all unrighteousness.

2. [Kathleen R. Wheeler?] "A New Leaf," quoted in The World's Best-Loved Poems, comp. James Gilchrist Lawson (New York, N.Y.: Harper & Row, Publishers, 1955), p. 260.

David's confession in Psalm 51 grows out of the crimes committed in 2 Samuel 11. Read over that passage and list the sins David committed.

2 Samuel 11:2 _____

Verse 4 _____

Verses 6–13 _____

Verses 14–21 _____

More than nine months passed between David's crimes and his confession. During that time he was very hush-hush about his sin. Many think that Psalm 32 describes the period prior to David's confession. What were the effects that his silence had on him spiritually, emotionally, and physically (vv. 3–4)?

_____

_____

_____

_____

_____

What was the catalyst for David's finally going public with his sin and asking for forgiveness (2 Sam. 12:1–13a)?

_____

_____

What consequences did he suffer (vv. 10–23)?

_____

_____

How was he shown mercy (v. 24)?

_____

_____

From Psalm 51, describe David's spiritual restoration.

_____

_____

_____

_____

How did David's spiritual restoration affect the consequences that Nathan prophesied in 2 Samuel 12:13?

_____

_____

Living Insights

Have you ever been in David's shoes? Ever been tempted to be unfaithful to Christ, with whom you knelt at the altar and committed yourself for eternity? Ever given yourself to something that compromised your fidelity to Him?

Describe the experience.

_____

_____

_____

Describe the consequences you endured because of it.

_____

_____

_____

Describe the catalyst that helped you realize your sin and brought you to your knees.

_____

_____

_____

Describe how you were shown mercy by God in your restoration.

_____

_____

_____

If that restoration is still incomplete, take a look at the following verses. They will certainly help the healing process. Psalm 103:1–14; Isaiah 1:18, 43:25, 44:21–23; 1 John 1:9.

Chapter 9

PREJUDICE IS A SIN

James 2:1–13

A young, single attorney once worked for a generous boss who gave all his employees a turkey every year at Thanksgiving. One year, before the birds were handed out, some of the attorney's co-workers replaced his real turkey with one made of papier-mâché. To make the bogus bird look and feel genuine, they wrapped it in brown paper, weighted it with lead, and added a real turkey neck and tail. On the Wednesday before Thanksgiving, the attorney went to the company boardroom, picked up his assigned turkey, and thanked his boss for his job and the bird.

Later, on the bus home, the young man wondered what to do with his prize. He didn't know how to cook it and couldn't possibly eat it all by himself. Before long, a rather run-down, discouraged-looking man got on the bus and sat next to the attorney. As they talked, the young man learned that the stranger had spent the entire day job hunting with no luck, that he had a large family, and that he was wondering what he would do about Thanksgiving the next day.

Suddenly the attorney was struck with an idea: Why not give his turkey to this man? But how? The fellow wasn't a freeloader and probably wouldn't accept charity. So the attorney asked, "How much money do you have?" "Oh, a couple of dollars and a few cents," the man answered. "Sold!" said the attorney and he put the turkey in the stranger's lap. Moved to tears, the stranger later got off the bus and waved good-bye, thrilled that his family would have a turkey for Thanksgiving.

The next Monday, the attorney's friends were dying to know about the turkey. You can imagine their dismay and the young attorney's horror when they both learned what each had done. For a week, the attorney and his co-workers rode the bus searching for the stranger they had unintentionally wronged, but they never found him.[1]

---

1. Charles R. Swindoll, *Three Steps Forward, Two Steps Back*, rev. ed. (Nashville, Tenn.: Thomas Nelson Publishers, 1990), pp. 23–25.

You can imagine how bad the attorney must have felt. But what about the stranger? Can you imagine what he thought, how he must have felt when he discovered the turkey was only a glob of paper? For all he knew, that young man had intentionally sold him a fake. Was he right? No. But the circumstantial evidence seemed to indicate that he was, and it would have been hard to convince him otherwise.

Like one of Aesop's fables, there's a moral behind this story: *It's impossible to judge another person's motives simply on the basis of outward appearance or any other external factor.* No one can determine the heart of another in a first-time encounter. That's why James says in chapter 2, verses 1–11, that prejudice and partiality are wrong!

Principle Stated

James presents his case against prejudice in a tightly constructed passage. First, he introduces a principle in verse 1, then he illustrates it in verses 2–4, explains it in verses 5–11 and, finally, applies it in verses 12–13. Let's listen now as James makes his opening statement.

> My brethren, do not hold your faith in our glorious Lord Jesus Christ with an attitude of personal favoritism. (v. 1)

Clearly stated, James' point is that faith in Christ and partiality are incompatible. The word *favoritism* used here comes from two words in the Greek which, when put together, mean "to receive by face." It's the idea of judging others solely on external face values. Externals such as clothes, cars, or color.[2]

It's important to note that James is not condemning the kind of discernment that comes from a thorough understanding of another's character. What he is dealing with here is our tendency to be prejudiced toward others because of superficial judgments based on outward appearances.

The Principle Illustrated

Following the statement of his principle, James fleshes out the issue with a vivid illustration.

---

2. The same term for *favoritism* used here is found in only three other places in the New Testament. In each passage, we're assured that the Father is not a respecter of persons. When He judges, He judges the heart, not outward appearances.

The Setting

> A man comes into your assembly with a gold ring
> and dressed in fine clothes, and there also comes in
> a poor man in dirty clothes. (v. 2)

Imagine, James says, you're the usher at a worship service and
in comes Mr. Have followed by Mr. Have-Not. The former is bedecked in gold rings and fine fabrics studded with jewels, while the
latter wears ragged hand-me-downs caked with dirt. What will you do?

The Response

> [If] you pay special attention to the one who is wear-
> ing the fine clothes, and say, "You sit here in a good
> place," and you say to the poor man, "You stand
> over there, or sit down by my footstool," . . . (v. 3)

According to Matthew 23:6, there were "chief seats" in the
synagogue, places of honor that the Pharisees loved to sit in. Now,
if we escorted the rich man down front and denied the poor man
a seat anywhere except in a far back corner, wouldn't our motive
be something less than pure?

The Motive

> Have you not made distinctions among yourselves,
> and become judges with evil motives? (v. 4)

Two things are clarified in this verse. First, *what was done:* The
usher "made distinctions." He discriminated based on appearances,
exalting one and mistreating another. Second, we're told *why it was
done:* because of evil motives . . . motives such as catering to the
rich, in hopes of selfish gain or to maintain class distinctions or
simply out of pride and contempt.

Principle Explained

Next, James presents three reasons why prejudice is wrong.
The first reason he gives is theological: *Prejudice is inconsistent
with God's methods.*

> Listen, my beloved brethren: did not God choose
> the poor of this world to be rich in faith and heirs
> of the kingdom which He promised to those who
> love Him? (v. 5)

Is James saying that God is partial toward the financially poor? No, of course not. As William Barclay has noted, "The great characteristic of God is his complete impartiality."[3] Barclay goes on to explain,

> James is not shutting the door on the rich—far from that. He is saying that the gospel of Christ is specially dear to the poor and that in it there is a welcome for the man who has none to welcome him, and that through it there is a value set on the man whom the world regards as valueless.[4]

James is simply saying that, from God's perspective, the real issue is the condition of one's soul. God bases His choices on the heart, not the wallet.

The apostle Paul echoes James' point in 1 Corinthians 1:25–29.

> The foolishness of God is wiser than men, and the weakness of God is stronger than men.
> For consider your calling, brethren, that there were not many wise according to the flesh, not many mighty, not many noble; but God has chosen the foolish things of the world to shame the wise, and God has chosen the weak things of the world to shame the things which are strong, and the base things of the world and the despised, God has chosen, the things that are not, that He might nullify the things that are, that no man should boast before God.

James' second reason that prejudice is wrong is a logical one: *Prejudice ignores the universality of sin.*

> But you have dishonored the poor man. Is it not the rich who oppress you and personally drag you into court? Do they not blaspheme the fair name by which you have been called? (James 2:6–7)

Besides the fact that it was ludicrous to exalt the very people who persecuted them, James reminds his readers that by catering

3. William Barclay, *The Letters of James and Peter*, rev. ed., The Daily Study Bible series (Philadelphia, Pa.: Westminster Press, 1976), p. 63.

4. Barclay, *Letters of James and Peter*, p. 67.

to the rich, they were denying that the wealthy are sinners and need the grace of God like all the rest.

James' last reason rests on the authority of the Bible: *Prejudice is sinful because it is inconsistent with Scripture.*

> If, however, you are fulfilling the royal law, according to the Scripture, "You shall love your neighbor as yourself," you are doing well. But if you show partiality, you are committing sin and are convicted by the law as transgressors. (vv. 8–9)

Centuries before, Moses said in Leviticus 19:18, "You shall love your neighbor as yourself." That was the law then, and it still is today. But if you show partiality, then you have sinned and become a lawbreaker. As one commentator observed,

> Anyone who shows favoritism breaks the supreme law of love for his neighbor, the law that comprehends all laws governing one's relationships to one's fellowmen.[5]

Wouldn't it be nice if all our relationships were guided by the royal law of love? But the fact is, we all have certain built-in prejudices that color our reactions to people. Some hold prejudices against divorced people or people who have been emotionally ill or those who belong to a different political, ethnic, or religious background.

These kinds of prejudices produce cliques, gossip mongers, legalists, and power-hungry groups in churches who put enormous pressure on others to conform to their rules of behavior. Each group has its own unwritten royal law of love that states, "We'll love you if you don't speak with an accent . . . if you dress a certain way . . . if you're educated . . . if . . . if . . . if." The list is endless.

Now, for some of us, James' condemnation of prejudice may seem a little too harsh. We think, "Sure, our love may have a few limitations, but at least we're not murderers!" James knew some would react this way, so he wrote the following. Listen.

> For whoever keeps the whole law and yet stumbles in one point, he has become guilty of all. For He who said, "Do not commit adultery," also said, "Do

5. Donald W. Burdick, "James," in *The Expositor's Bible Commentary*, ed. Frank E. Gaebelein (Grand Rapids, Mich.: Zondervan Publishing House, Regency Reference Library, 1981), vol. 12, p. 180.

not commit murder." Now if you do not commit
adultery, but do commit murder, you have become
a transgressor of the law. (James 2:10–11)

While it's true that some sins are more heinous than others, it
is not true that we're any less guilty of breaking God's law simply
because we only show partiality instead of committing murder.

Principle Applied

In verses 12–13 James brings his thoughts on prejudice to a close
with three basic principles for us to apply.

First: *Let the Scriptures—not your heritage—be your standard.*

So speak and so act, as those who are to be judged
by the law of liberty. (v. 12)

Instead of excusing your prejudices with statements like, "That's
the way I was brought up," or, "That's just the way I am," allow
God to change how you think, speak, and act by living according
to His Word.

Second: *Let love be your law.* Some of the neediest people typically receive the worst kinds of prejudiced responses. Before you
respond to someone, think first, "How can I love this person?
What's needed to help build this person up?"

Third: *Let mercy be your message.*

For judgment will be merciless to one who has shown
no mercy; mercy triumphs over judgment. (v. 13)

A prejudiced person cannot help but be judgmental. But the
individual who is motivated by the law of love will exude mercy in
their relationships.

How would you respond if you suddenly discovered that your
closest friend had a background like the woman at the well or the
apostle Paul?[6] Would it change your love? Probably not. Then why
are we so quick to condemn others with similar backgrounds whom
we hardly even know? The reason, James says, is prejudice.

Unlike an Aesop fable, our lives are real stories that are constantly read by the people around us. What will be the moral behind
your story? The law of love or the sin of prejudice?

6. See John 4:5–18 and Acts 7:58–8:3.

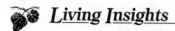

Living Insights

Prejudice. Our English word stems from a Latin noun that emphasizes a prejudgment of someone, causing us to form an opinion without knowing the facts. Once we've raced to our conclusions, ignoring the facts, we're well on our way to irrational thinking—thinking that results in an insidious attitude that says, "Don't bother me with the truth, my mind is made up." The whole point of James 2:1–13 is to diffuse this kind of faulty thinking. Read through the text once more and probe the spirit of prejudice. Then describe in the space provided why prejudice causes the following to clash head-on.

Faith and favoritism (v. 1): _____

_____

_____

_____

_____

The wealthy and the poor (vv. 2–7): _____

_____

_____

_____

_____

Self and neighbor (vv. 8–11): _____

_____

_____

_____

_____

Mercy and judgment (vv. 12–13): _____

_____

_____

_____

_____

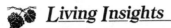

Now let's turn the spotlight away from James' list and focus it on other prejudices you have observed operating in the world today. List those prejudices.

1. _____

2. _____

3. _____

4. _____

5. _____

Which of these biases apply to you? Does one grip you more than any other? Describe your struggle with it.

_____

_____

From what you've read in James, write down the scriptural principle that is most apt to turn your thinking toward healthy opinions.

_____

_____

Finally, formulate the steps you plan to take the next time you recognize personal prejudice. You may want to begin this way:

When I recognize my prejudice, I will

a. *tell myself that I lack sound information and am prejudging that person, which makes my opinion irrational and unfair.*

b. _____

_____

_____

c. _____

_____

_____

Chapter 10

HOW TO DISCERN
WITHOUT JUDGING
1 Samuel 16:1–13

Judging is a prickly subject, isn't it? Why? Because we tend to be either quick to judge others, which is bad, or quick to condemn others who judge, which can also be bad.

"But I thought James said it was wrong to judge others." You're right . . . but. James only condemned the kind of judging that involves prejudice—judging with evil motives. There's another way to judge, one with good motives which the Lord actually encourages His children to practice.

When Solomon asked God for "an understanding heart to judge Thy people to discern between good and evil" (1 Kings 3:9a), he wasn't rebuked for requesting something sinful; God rewarded Solomon for seeking something wise.

> And God said to him, "Because you have asked this thing and have not asked for yourself long life, nor have asked riches for yourself, nor have you asked for the life of your enemies, but have asked for your-self discernment to understand justice, behold, I have done according to your words. Behold, I have given you a wise and discerning heart." (vv. 11–12a)

But Solomon wasn't the only one who judged. Joseph, Jesus, the apostles—they all judged others too. In fact, the Scriptures teach that every mature Christian possesses the important ability to judge—to practice discernment. Let's take a few minutes to examine what God says about judging with discernment, so that you can cultivate this indispensable quality too.

The Biblical Account

To begin, let's survey 1 Samuel 16:1–13 and then draw out some insights and principles that we can apply.

Historical Situation

When you open your Bible to 1 Samuel 16, you are stepping back in time to the era when Saul was king over Israel. Saul disobeyed God, however, so the Lord dispatched the prophet Samuel to select a new king.

> Now the Lord said to Samuel, "How long will you grieve over Saul, since I have rejected him from being king over Israel? Fill your horn with oil, and go; I will send you to Jesse the Bethlehemite, for I have selected a king for Myself among his sons." But Samuel said, "How can I go? When Saul hears of it, he will kill me." And the Lord said, "Take a heifer with you, and say, 'I have come to sacrifice to the Lord.' And you shall invite Jesse to the sacrifice, and I will show you what you shall do; and you shall anoint for Me the one whom I designate to you." So Samuel did what the Lord said, and came to Bethlehem. And the elders of the city came trembling to meet him and said, "Do you come in peace?" And he said, "In peace; I have come to sacrifice to the Lord. Consecrate yourselves and come with me to the sacrifice." He also consecrated Jesse and his sons, and invited them to the sacrifice. (vv. 1–5)

In addition to being a prophet, Samuel also served as the nation's judge, visiting various communities to settle disputes, confront sins, and offer sacrifices for the people. Though he was the most respected man in Israel, Samuel still feared that Saul would kill him if he knew of his mission to anoint a new king. So God explained to Samuel how he could avoid rousing Saul's wrath by selecting a new king while he performed his usual duties in Bethlehem.

Individual Examination

Following the sacrifice, Samuel went with his special guests, Jesse and his sons, to their home. There they celebrated a customary sacrificial meal together, and Samuel prepared to anoint Israel's next king. According to verse 6, as soon as Samuel entered Jesse's home his eyes fell on the oldest son, Eliab.

> Then it came about when they entered, that he looked at Eliab and thought, "Surely the Lord's anointed is before Him."

Eliab must have been a stunning young man to attract Samuel's attention like that. But Samuel's judgment of Eliab was a superficial one. It was made in an instant, "when they entered," and it was based solely on outward appearances such as height, weight, and looks. Exactly the kind of favoritism, "receiving by face," James warned us about (see James 2:1). Before Samuel could say a word, however, God taught His prophet the difference between superficial judging and discernment.

> But the Lord said to Samuel, "Do not look at his appearance or at the height of his stature, because I have rejected him; for God sees not as man sees, for man looks at the outward appearance, but the Lord looks at the heart." (v. 7)

The Hebrew reads, "For man looks to the eyes, but Jehovah looks to the heart." Samuel got the message and immediately passed over Eliab to look at Jesse's other sons.

> Then Jesse called Abinadab, and made him pass before Samuel. And he said, "Neither has the Lord chosen this one." Next Jesse made Shammah pass by. And he said, "Neither has the Lord chosen this one." Thus Jesse made seven of his sons pass before Samuel. But Samuel said to Jesse, "The Lord has not chosen these." (vv. 8–10)

Final Selection

Seven sons and still no king. But God said there would be a king, so Samuel asks,

> "Are these all the children?" And he said, "There remains yet the youngest, and behold, he is tending the sheep." Then Samuel said to Jesse, "Send and bring him; for we will not sit down until he comes here." (v. 11)

Jesse had overlooked David entirely. You cannot help but suspect that this father had failed to recognize his youngest son's potential. Samuel had certainly become aware, and he refused to let anyone sit and eat until David had been brought in.

> So he sent and brought him in. Now he was ruddy, with beautiful eyes and a handsome appearance. And the Lord said, "Arise, anoint him; for this is he." (v. 12)

This is David's first appearance in the Scriptures. Notice what is said about him. The word *ruddy* means reddish, which probably referred to the color of his hair. Why mention this? Because it was considered a mark of beauty to have auburn hair among a people whose hair was predominantly black. And verse 12 also says that David had beautiful eyes and was handsome in appearance.

It was an emotional moment. Samuel was staring at Israel's next king, a boy whose only experience at leading had been over a flock of woolly subjects. Yet the prophet didn't hesitate to trust in God's judgment of David's heart, and so Samuel fulfilled the mission he had come for.

> Then Samuel took the horn of oil and anointed him in the midst of his brothers; and the Spirit of the Lord came mightily upon David from that day forward. And Samuel arose and went to Ramah. (v. 13)

Additional Insights

Now that we're familiar with the overall story of 1 Samuel 16:1–13, let's go back and draw out four specific insights.

First: *Mistakes are made when we judge quickly on surface evidence.* Samuel made two mistakes when he first saw Eliab (v. 6). First, he made a snap judgment and, second, he made a surface judgment. These are the same two mistakes the Israelites made in choosing Saul to be their first king. They saw that he was taller than everyone else and immediately roared their approval, "Long live the king!" (1 Sam. 10:22–24). Samuel knew how pitifully wrong their hasty assessment had been—Saul had been a disaster as king. And yet, the prophet turned right around and made the same mistake with his own hurried evaluation of Eliab. Fortunately, the Lord intervened this time, teaching Samuel to base his judgments on the heart, not on someone's height.

Second: *Looking at the heart is against our nature.* God underscored this when he told Samuel, in verse 7, that our natural tendency is to judge people by their outward appearances. But we can change. It may not be easy or happen quickly, but it is possible in the Lord. When we grow spiritually, taking on His heart and perspective, a new nature blossoms, one whose natural tendency always prompts us to look to the heart.

Third: *People who are significant to God are often insignificant to others.* David was one of those people. When Samuel arrived to select a king from among Jesse's sons, David was left out with the sheep (v. 11). He was completely overlooked by his father, the one person you would expect to be aware of his son's potential. The qualities of David's heart, however, didn't go unnoticed by the Lord.

Fourth: *Appearance is important.* Did you notice the first thing we learned about David after he was brought before Samuel? It was his appearance (v. 12).

Doesn't it seem interesting that, after emphasizing to Samuel not to judge others by their appearance, God would then focus first on how David looked rather than tell us what was in his heart? Perhaps the reason is simply that our appearance *is* important. Certainly it's not the basis for judging character or a sign of spirituality or more important than the heart. But it is important. How we take care of our bodies and present ourselves in public reflects on our Lord.

First Samuel 16:1–13 is a great story, and the insights gleaned from it are helpful, but still we haven't dealt directly with the question, What's the difference between judging in the wrong sense, as Samuel initially did, and discerning in the right sense? To find out, let's turn our attention to a couple of New Testament passages.

Probably the most familiar passage in Scripture dealing with the topic of judging is found in Matthew 7:1, "Do not judge lest you be judged." The word *judge* used here in Greek is *krinō*, meaning "to separate, select so as to declare a verdict." This type of judging is wrong because of the motive or attitude behind the judging. Jesus probably had the Pharisees in mind when He said this. They were a smugly self-righteous bunch whose judgments were characteristically harsh, superficial, and never motivated out of a real concern to help the other person.

Now let's find out what *discernment,* judging the right way, means. Hebrews 5:14 states,

> But solid food is for the mature, who because of practice have their senses trained to discern good and evil.

The term for *discern* used here is *diakrinō*. It's the same Greek word for *judge* that Jesus used in Matthew 7, but with a prefix added. Now the term means "to separate, to distinguish, to select." It's the idea of distinguishing on the basis of comparison, coupled with careful thinking. The mark of a mature Christian is the ability to discern good from evil, to distinguish strengths from weaknesses, to be concerned for the welfare of those we correct.

Some Practical Principles

Discernment is a great skill which, if used wrongly, can wreak great harm. Each of us, with God's help, must wrestle with where we will draw our own lines between discernment and judgment. And though we cannot say how and where that line should be drawn for you, here are four practical principles that can at least help you know *when* to use discernment.

Discernment is essential:

1. *when prolonged involvement is being considered.* For example, we should exercise discernment when choosing a roommate, an intimate friend, a business partner, or a spouse. Perhaps you're trying to choose a new church, a new job, or a financial partner in a big investment. God is pleased when we judge with discernment before we jump into anything that involves a prolonged commitment.

2. *when there are fractures in the body of Christ.* Galatians 6:1 and James 5:19–20 both talk about this particular situation.

> Brethren, even if a man is caught in any trespass, you who are spiritual, restore such a one in a spirit of gentleness; each one looking to yourself, lest you too be tempted. (Gal. 6:1)
>
> My brethren, if any among you strays from the truth, and one turns him back, let him know that he who turns a sinner from the error of his way will save his soul from death, and will cover a multitude of sins. (James 5:19–20)

The word *restore* in Galatians 6:1 is a medical term for healing a broken bone or mending a torn net. If a friend is clearly violating God's Word, we're to go to that individual and help mend that person's life. This is the kind of compassionate discernment God honors, the kind motivated by love and a genuine care for the other person.

3. *when leadership positions are being considered.* In many churches, leadership elections are, unfortunately, nothing more than popularity contests. Where you would expect people to carefully apply discernment, snap judgments abound, instead, based on whoever is the best liked or most visible.

In 1 Timothy 5:22 the apostle Paul cautions his young friend not to be hasty in placing others in positions of leadership, which in that day was effected by the laying on of hands.

> Do not lay hands upon anyone too hastily and thus
> share responsibility for the sins of others; keep your-
> self free from sin. (v. 22)

Choosing a leader isn't a matter of expedience, popularity, or availability. It's a matter of discernment—or the lack of it.

4. *when distinguishing truth from error.* Paul again counsels Timothy,

> If anyone advocates a different doctrine, and does
> not agree with sound words, those of our Lord Jesus
> Christ, and with the doctrine conforming to godli-
> ness, he is conceited and understands nothing; but
> he has a morbid interest in controversial questions
> and disputes about words, out of which arise envy,
> strife, abusive language, evil suspicions, and con-
> stant friction between men of depraved mind and
> deprived of the truth, who suppose that godliness is
> a means of gain. (1 Tim. 6:3–5)

Discerning truth from error was also on the disciple John's heart when he commanded us to "test the spirits to see whether they are from God" (1 John 4:1). Not only are we to be discerning about people, but also about what they teach, making sure it is consistent with the Scriptures.

Concluding Thought

Remember this trick question your parents used on you when you were little: "You want to grow up to be big and strong, don't you?" You proudly said yes, of course, and without knowing it you sprang the trap. "Well, then, you've got to eat your vegetables." Gasp! Too late you realized you had sealed your own fate, with no way out.

According to Hebrews 5:14, to grow up big and strong, as mature Christians, we've all got to practice discernment. And you do want to grow up to be big and strong—and discerning—like Solomon, don't you? Ah ha! Got you!

 Living Insights STUDY ONE

To be discerning without being judgmental is a crucial ability that the body of Christ must learn if we are to effectively nurture others. And the New Testament agrees. As you think through the

following passages, lift a principle or two from each that touch on the art of developing biblical discernment.

Romans 14 _____

_____

_____

_____

_____

1 Corinthians 5 _____

_____

_____

_____

_____

Colossians 2:16–23 _____

_____

_____

_____

_____

🍇 *Living Insights*   STUDY TWO

Even Samuel, a prophet of God, got caught in the trap of judging on the basis of externals (1 Sam. 16:1–5). But let's not be too hasty in judging him ourselves! Instead, put yourself in Samuel's place (vv. 6–13). Begin to struggle, as he did, with the responsibility he had to shoulder. Try to imagine the way he must have been thinking. What do you think his perspective was?

_____

_____

_____

_____

In contrast to Samuel's viewpoint, what perspective did God bring to the situation?

_____

_____

_____

_____

How about Jesse—how would you describe his perspective?

_____

_____

_____

_____

From each of these vantage points, what principles can you derive that will help sharpen *your* discernment skills?

_____

_____

_____

_____

Chapter 11

YOU CAN'T HAVE ONE WITHOUT THE OTHER

James 2:14–26

Someone once said that faith is like calories: you can't see them, but you can always see their results! And that is the major theme resonating throughout James' letter—*results*. Genuine faith produces genuine works. And nowhere is this theme more passionately argued than in James 2:14–26.

Initial Clarification

Before we begin our study, there is one issue that needs clarification. And that is the apparent contradiction between the thrust of our passage today: "a man is justified by works, and not by faith alone" (2:24); and Paul's great thesis in Romans 3–5: "a man is justified by faith apart from works of the Law" (Rom. 3:28; see also Eph. 2:8–9; 2 Tim. 1:9; Titus 3:5).

It was this same issue that caused Martin Luther to label James a "right strawy epistle,"[1] meaning that he felt it lacked solid, biblical doctrine. To Luther, whose battle cry in the Reformation was "Justification by faith alone," James' battle cry of "Justification by works" was blatant heresy. But is it, really? To find out, let's examine three important differences between Paul and James.

First, it's important to understand that the *emphasis* of Paul's and James' writings are different. Paul stresses the root of salvation, which is faith in Christ plus nothing. James calls attention to the fruit *after* salvation. Every believer rooted in Christ by faith will bear fruit, like branches on a vine (see John 15:4–5). Paul talks about the root, James talks about the fruit.

A second contrast between Paul and James is *perspective*. Paul looks at life from God's perspective, while James looks at life from a human perspective. Paul sees the fire in the fireplace, while James

---

1. Quoted by J. Ronald Blue, "James," in *The Bible Knowledge Commentary*, New Testament ed., John F. Walvoord and Roy B. Zuck, eds. (Wheaton, Ill.: SP Publications, Victor Books, 1983), p. 815.

eyes the smoke coming out the chimney. To James, the world should be able to tell that a faith burns in our hearts by the works they see coming out in our lives.

The third contrast, and perhaps the most important one, is the difference in *terms*. Both Paul and James use the same word, *justified*, but with two different meanings. When Paul mentions justification, he means the act of God at salvation whereby He declares the believing sinner righteous while still in a sinning state. James, on the other hand, uses it to mean "validate or evidence." We justify or prove our faith, James says, by our works.

Perhaps commentator W. H. Griffith Thomas reconciled these two ideas best when he wrote,

> It has been well said that St. Paul and St. James are not soldiers of different armies fighting against each other, but soldiers of the same army fighting back to back against enemies coming from opposite directions.[2]

James strawy? No. If understood properly, James' letter is as solidly biblical and practical as they come.

Expositional Study

Our passage today is also as feisty as they come in the New Testament. James has a bone to pick—one that he has been building up to since he opened his letter and that he will continue to underscore till he closes.

Introductory Question

To introduce the cardinal passage of his letter, James asks two rhetorical questions that not only beg an answer but also an analysis.

> What use is it, my brethren, if a man says he
> has faith, but he has not works? (2:14a)

What good does it do, asks James, to say you have faith if you have no works to justify that claim? It's like asking, What good is it to have a driver's license if you don't drive? Answer? None. So what good is a faith that doesn't produce works? You guessed it. After pointing out the worthlessness of a workless faith, James then asks an even deeper question, "Can that faith save him?" (v. 14b).

---

2. W. H. Griffith Thomas, *St. Paul's Epistle to the Romans: A Devotional Commentary* (Grand Rapids, Mich.: William B. Eerdmans Publishing Co., 1947), vol. 1, p. 132.

In Greek, questions can be framed in two different ways. One phrasing expects a positive answer, and the other, like James' second question, expects a negative answer. Essentially, he's asking, Can that kind of phony faith save? And the answer, of course, is no. The great leaders of the Reformation used to say we are justified by faith alone, but not by the faith which is alone. Genuine, saving faith is accompanied by fruit; it is not found in the empty wastes of hollow words.

Characteristics of Genuine Faith

Next, in verses 15–20, James illustrates four marks of genuine faith.

First: *It is not indifferent . . . but involved.*

> If a brother or sister is without clothing and in need of daily food, and one of you says to them, "Go in peace, be warmed and be filled," and yet you do not give them what is necessary for their body, what use is that? (vv. 15–16)

This illustration is easy to understand because, in one way or another, most of us have been that needy person and can still remember the empty platitudes we received instead of real help. Listen to how one commentator translates the emotionally detached response given in verse 16.

> Keep up your spirits, don't become discouraged; someone will yet come to your relief; go away from my presence comforted.[3]

What is missing? James says it's the proof of genuine faith—real food and real clothes. No one echoes this point better than the apostle John.

> But whoever has the world's goods, and beholds his brother in need and closes his heart against him, how does the love of God abide in him? Little children, let us not love with word or with tongue, but in deed and truth. (1 John 3:17–18)

Second: *Genuine faith is not independent . . . but in partnership.*

---

3. Curtis Vaughan, *James: A Study Guide* (Grand Rapids, Mich.: Zondervan Publishing House, 1969), p. 61.

> Even so faith, if it has no works, is dead, being by
> itself. (James 2:17)

There was a song made popular years ago titled, "Love and Marriage." Remember the beginning? "Love and marriage, love and marriage, go together like a horse and carriage." And on it went, concluding in the final stanza with the words, "You can't have one without the other."[4] Faith and works go together like a horse and carriage also. You can't have one without the other. Dissolve the partnership and faith dies. Faith was never designed to dwell alone, separate from the partner that proves its existence.

Third: *Genuine faith is not invisible . . . but on display.* James illustrates this by creating an imaginary conversation between two people. The one speaking in verse 18 agrees with James.

> But someone may well say, "You have faith, and I
> have works; show me your faith without the works,
> and I will show you my faith by my works." (v. 18)

The word *show* means to bring to light, to display or exhibit. James' imaginary friend is talking about demonstrating genuine faith. "Do your best to show me your faith without using works, and I'll demonstrate my faith by my works. We'll see which one of us really has the genuine item."

Some might argue, however, "Look, there are all kinds of Christians. Some have the gift of works, others are quiet, never displaying their faith." But that's like saying some people have the gift of breathing and others don't! We delude ourselves if we think it doesn't matter whether we evidence our faith or not. James' whole point is that if it doesn't show, you don't have it.

Fourth: *Genuine faith is not intellectual . . . but from the heart.* Next James picks on the other imaginary partner in the conversation, someone we might call a religious intellectual.

> You believe that God is one. (v. 19a)

This person's defense against not having any works is to hide behind an impressive knowledge of God's Word. "My theology is impeccable; I believe God is One, just like it says in Deuteronomy 6:4." "Wonderful," James says, "join hands with the demons."

---

4. Sammy Cahn, "Love and Marriage," as quoted in *Songs with Lyrics by Sammy Cahn* (Ft. Lauderdale, Fla.: Cahn Music Co., 1955).

You do well; the demons also believe, and shudder. (v. 19b)

The demons have their religious facts straight, but they're still demons. We can know all the religious facts we want, but until we believe in Christ, we're no more Christian than the demons.

There is one interesting difference between our intellectual friend and the demons, however. James says that the demonic tribes tremble at the thought of God. The Greek term used for *shudder* suggests a "rough, uneven surface." They get goose pimples! But the dead faith of the religious intellectual doesn't produce even that much of a reaction.

Now James is not ridiculing having an intelligent faith; rather, he's mocking those religious intellectuals who love to debate religious truth but have no plans whatsoever to commit themselves to following Jesus Christ.

Next, James invites his imaginary religious intellectual to learn a hard fact about his faith.

But are you willing to recognize, you foolish fellow, that faith without works is useless? (v. 20)

If you take away the element of application, you're left only with mere intellectual assent, which neither glorifies God nor helps the person who possesses it.

Examples of Genuine Faith

To emphasize that genuine faith is evidenced by good works, James now directs our attention to Abraham and Rahab.

Was not Abraham our father justified by works, when he offered up Isaac his son on the altar? You see that faith was working with his works, and as a result of the works, faith was perfected; and the Scripture was fulfilled which says, "And Abraham believed God, and it was reckoned to him as righteousness," and he was called the friend of God. You see that a man is justified by works, and not by faith alone. And in the same way was not Rahab the harlot also justified by works, when she received the messengers and sent them out by another way? (vv. 21–25)

James couldn't have picked two more opposite people as proof that our works prove our faith. Abraham was the father of the Jews;

Rahab was a pagan prostitute. Abraham was moral, admired, a Jewish patriarch; Rahab was a harlot, looked on with disdain, considered insignificant. And yet both evidenced the same kind of faith. Abraham "justified," proved his faith, by offering up his son Isaac (see Gen. 22), and Rahab demonstrated her faith when she risked her life to protect two Israelite spies (see Josh. 2).

Concluding Principle

Finally, James summarizes his entire discussion in verse 26.

> For just as the body without the spirit is dead, so also faith without works is dead.

The concluding principle is simple. When there is separation, there is death. It's true physically, when the soul separates from the body; and it's true spiritually, when faith is separated from works. Without works, faith is nothing but a corpse, void of vitality and useless to everybody but the undertaker.

Faith, like calories, cannot be seen, but James says that you can always see its results. What results do others see in your life? Take a moment to think back over the characteristics of genuine faith and compare them with your own.

Genuine faith is involved . . . is yours? Genuine faith is a partnership . . . is yours? Genuine faith is displayed . . . is yours? Genuine faith is from the heart . . . is yours?

Remember, James isn't saying that our salvation is dependent on our works. Nor is he trying to make us produce more works out of guilt or fear. He's only questioning those who claim to believe in Christ but whose lives never show any evidence of that faith. "If you say that you're saved, why doesn't your life show it?" It's a fair question and a penetrating one. James says you'd better think about it, your "faith" may not have a heavenly pulse.

 Living Insights

Abraham's faith caused God to declare him righteous (see Gen. 15:6; Rom. 4:1–3). Describe what was going on in Abraham's life when he was justified by faith (see Gen. 15).

_____

_____

James puts the spotlight on Abraham's life thirty years after God had declared Abraham righteous, and he shows us how Abraham visibly demonstrated his faith by his behavior (Gen. 22:9–10, 12, 16). Examine these verses and explain how this event is different from his encounter with God in Genesis 15:6.

_____

_____

_____

Rahab's justification by faith is also connected to a historical event (see Heb. 11:31; Josh. 2). What turned her heart to God (see Josh. 2:11)?

_____

_____

Do some detective work in Joshua 2 and discover where in the text Rahab acts out her godly convictions, and jot the references here.

_____

Check your answer to the preceding note with James 2:25. Now try to see Rahab as God must have seen her. First, when she responds to Him as recorded in Joshua 2:11, this is justification by _____. Second, at a potential cost of her own life, Rahab sides with the Israelites. God observes her response to His people. Here she was justified by _____. In your own words, how do these two truths harmonize with one another?

_____

_____

_____

_____

_____

Have you been putting on weight lately, spiritually speaking? Contrary to our physical bodies, our souls are always better off gaining weight than losing it. As Solomon noted,

> The soul of the sluggard craves and gets nothing,
> But the soul of the diligent is made fat. (Prov. 13:4)

Use this time to count the calories of your faith. On a scale of one to ten, one being malnourished and ten being well-fed, rate how well you are evidencing the genuine characteristics of faith.

Genuine faith is not indifferent but involved.

1 2 3 4 5 6 7 8 9 10

Genuine faith is not independent but in partnership.

1 2 3 4 5 6 7 8 9 10

Genuine faith is not invisible but on display.

1 2 3 4 5 6 7 8 9 10

Genuine faith is not intellectual but from the heart.

1 2 3 4 5 6 7 8 9 10

Which of these areas needs some fattening up in your life?

_____

With this area in mind, take a moment now to begin developing a new diet for your soul. Bon appétit!

_____

_____

_____

_____

Chapter 12
JUSTIFIED BY WORKS
Genesis 22:1–14

Alan Redpath, in his biography of David, observed:

> The conversion of a soul is the miracle of a
> moment, the manufacture of a saint is the task of
> a lifetime.[1]

In our last lesson, James referred to one of the most revered
saints in all the Bible when he asked,

> Was not Abraham our father justified by works, when
> he offered up Isaac his son on the altar? (James 2:21)

This question contains the key to the manufacturing of Abraham
from a callow convert into a steadfast saint: *testing.*

Time and again God put Abraham through the furnace of testing,
each time with the plan of fashioning him into a stable man of God,
a man who would forever be known as "the friend of God" (v. 23).

Let's step back in time now, pausing to look at some of the first
painful tests Abraham had to endure. Then we'll take a deep breath
and climb the slopes of Mount Moriah to examine the worst crisis
in that saintly patriarch's life.

Survey of Four Crises in Abraham's Life

One thing we need to understand before we turn to these crises
is the reason behind them. God did not put Abraham to the test
to *see* if he was a believer but to *show* the validity of his faith. James
calls this being "justified by works" (v. 21), by which he means that
Abraham proved himself to be a genuine man of faith by his works
of obedience.

Now, on to the tests themselves.

The first major crisis came when God told Abraham to leave
his home (Gen. 12). At seventy-five, Abraham had to leave all

---

1. Alan Redpath, *The Making of a Man of God* (Westwood, N.J.: Fleming H. Revell Co.,
1962), p. 5.

that he knew and loved, everything that was familiar and dear to him, to set out for the unseen land of God's promise. "Home" disappeared behind him; a vast unknown stretched before him. But he trusted God, said his good-byes, and willingly turned his back on Ur forever.

Abraham's second crisis occurred when he separated from his nephew Lot (Gen. 13). Though there was strife between Lot's herdsmen and his, Abraham nevertheless loved his nephew and cared about his welfare. But he also had the wisdom to do what he knew was best, so he separated from the young man and waited for God's next step.

The third major crisis came when God told Abraham to abandon his cherished plans for his first son, Ishmael (Gen. 17; see also 21:8–14). It was through Isaac that God wanted to rain down his blessings on Abraham, not through the son of Sarah's handmaiden. And though Abraham yearned for God's blessings, he still had a father's love for his firstborn. Can you not hear the ache in the old man's voice as he entreats the Lord?

> And Abraham said to God, "Oh that Ishmael might live before Thee!" (17:18)

But despite his fatherly love, Abraham determined to follow God's way and not his own.

Now we come to the fourth crisis, the greatest test of all. Abraham must be obedient to the God who has just asked him to sacrifice his beloved son—his only son now that Ishmael is gone—Isaac (Gen. 22).

Study of the Final Crisis

Let's turn to Genesis 22 and briefly investigate this final test. In doing so, we'll get a clearer picture of what is involved in being manufactured into a saint of God.

Revelation of the Test

> Now it came about after these things, that God tested Abraham, and said to him, "Abraham!" And he said, "Here I am." And He said, "Take now your son, your only son, whom you love, Isaac, and go to the land of Moriah; and offer him there as a burnt offering on one of the mountains of which I will tell you." (vv. 1–2)

The word *tested* in verse 1 is an intense form of the word in the original Hebrew. Used only here in the entire book of Genesis, it is actually saying that God *intensely* tested Abraham—that this was to be a test like no other.

By the way, there are times when God's tests are intense for us as well. Maybe you have just come through such an experience; perhaps that lies ahead of you. Wherever you are, there is hope in remembering this truth: God not only plans the length of our tests, He plans their depth as well. And He knows just how much we can endure (see Ps. 103:14).

Back in our Genesis passage, notice the progression God uses to reveal just who He wants sacrificed (v. 2). From this sequence we are given a little window into the workings of Abraham's mind.

God:	Take now your son.
Abraham:	But I have two sons.
God:	Your only son.
Abraham:	Well, each is the only son of his mother.
God:	Whom you love.
Abraham:	Hmmm. I do love Ishmael.
God:	ISAAC!

End of conversation.

To fully appreciate the emotional impact of this scene, you must remember that, by this time, Abraham was well over a hundred years old. He and Sarah had waited many years for the arrival of this son of promise, and it was only through him that God's blessings would come to fruition. How Abraham must have loved this child, and how he must have reeled to think of laying his son on an altar as a burnt offering!

The Hebrew word used here for "offering," *'olah*, refers to a whole burnt offering, which would have included an animal's hooves, face, head, skin—*everything*. The entire animal would be consumed in smoke, and this is just what God has told Abraham to do with Isaac. A deep test indeed.[2]

2. "The 'burnt-offering,' (*'olah*), is the type of sacrifice best suited for this purpose, because it typifies complete surrender to God. The term is derived from the root *'alah*, signifying 'to go up,' i.e., in the smoke of the sacrifice. Therefore, the son given to Abraham is to be given back to Yahweh without reservations of any sort." H. C. Leupold, *Exposition of Genesis* (Grand Rapids, Mich.: Baker Book House, 1942), vol. 2, p. 621.

Response of Abraham

Verses 3–10 reveal four characteristics of Abraham's response, the first of which is found in verse 3.

> So Abraham rose early in the morning and saddled his donkey, and took two of his young men with him and Isaac his son; and he split wood for the burnt offering, and arose and went to the place of which God had told him.

Did you notice it? He "rose *early in the morning.*" No procrastinating, no delays. Abraham's obedience was *immediate.*

How immediate are your responses to God? Do you sometimes find yourself piddling around and stalling with that old standby, "I'll do it in a little while"? Keep in mind that one of Satan's most successful strategies is procrastination, getting us to drag our feet when we know we've had a clear command from God. Why not thwart the enemy of your soul by following Abraham's example instead?

Another aspect of Abraham's response was that it was *characterized by faith.*

> On the third day Abraham raised his eyes and saw the place from a distance. And Abraham said to his young men, "Stay here with the donkey, and I and the lad will go yonder; and we will worship and *return to you.*" (vv. 4–5, emphasis added)

What a remarkable statement! With the mountain of sacrifice looming in the distance, Abraham was able to focus on worshiping the Lord and trusting in His ability even to raise the dead, if it came to that (see Heb. 11:19). And not one note of remorse, despondency, regret, or bitterness was sounded in all this symphony of obedient faithfulness.

Perhaps you've read this definition of faith: "Faith sees the invisible, believes the incredible, and receives the impossible."[3] It certainly applies to Abraham. He saw what couldn't be seen, believed in the unbelievable, and eagerly waited for God to achieve the impossible. He knew that impossibilities are God's specialty. Do you?

---

3. Quoted in *Encyclopedia of 7,700 Illustrations,* ed. and comp. Paul Lee Tan (n.p.: Assurance Publishers, 1979), p. 405.

Leaving the servants behind, Abraham and Isaac began their slow ascent up Mount Moriah.

> And Abraham took the wood of the burnt offering and laid it on Isaac his son, and he took in his hand the fire and the knife. So the two of them walked on together. And Isaac spoke to Abraham his father and said, "My father!" And he said, "Here I am, my son." And he said, "Behold, the fire and the wood, but where is the lamb for the burnt offering?" And Abraham said, "God will provide for Himself the lamb for the burnt offering, my son." So the two of them walked on together. (Gen. 22:6–8)

"God will provide." In this compassionate and hope-filled answer, we find the third facet of Abraham's response: it was *based on the character of God.* God had promised that through Isaac Abraham's descendants would be named (21:12), and this obedient father was staking his whole future on his Lord's unchangeable nature.

The fourth characteristic of Abraham's response was that it was *thorough and complete.* Just look at all of the preparations he carried out: he "saddled his donkey," "split wood" (22:3); "took the wood," "took in his hand the fire and the knife" (v. 6); "built the altar," "arranged the wood," "bound his son Isaac," "laid him on the altar" (v. 9); "stretched out his hand," and "took the knife to slay his son" (v. 10). His obedience didn't shrink from a single detail.

And God rewarded him for his unflinching faith.

Reward of God

With his son, his only son, whom he loved, Isaac, bound and waiting on the altar, Abraham raised the knife to plunge it into the boy, when suddenly

> the angel of the Lord called to him from heaven,
> and said, "Abraham, Abraham!"[4] (v. 11a)

Though he had come to that place in his walk with God where God meant more to him than Isaac, Abraham nevertheless must have cried out hoarsely, "Here I am," with a mixture of relief and strained waiting to see what God would do next (v. 11b).

---

4. In Hebrew, when a name is repeated, it is done so out of respect. This was as if God were saying, "I have no further need of proof. You have validated your faith."

And what God did next was to reward Abraham with the life of his son.

> "Do not stretch out your hand against the lad, and do nothing to him; for now I know that you fear God, since you have not withheld your son, your only son, from Me." (v. 12)

Notice the phrase, "Now I know that you fear God." This is what James was referring to when he said, "Was not Abraham our father justified by works"—in other words, did he not validate his faith—"when he offered up Isaac his son on the altar?" (James 2:21). God was telling Abraham that he had indeed proved his faith, that he was more than a convert now; he had become a true saint.

So now we have seen two of Abraham's rewards: his son was spared and his obedience was approved. But there is one more. A substitute was given, fulfilling Abraham's trust that God would provide.

> Then Abraham raised his eyes and looked, and behold, behind him a ram caught in the thicket by his horns; and Abraham went and took the ram, and offered him up for a burnt offering in the place of his son. (Gen. 22:13)

How Abraham's heart must have overflowed with praise and adoration for his merciful Lord! He was so moved by God's provision that he

> called the name of that place The Lord Will Provide, as it is said to this day, "In the mount of the Lord it will be provided." (v. 14)

And Abraham's exultation did not go unnoticed by God.

> Then the angel of the Lord called to Abraham a second time from heaven, and said, "By Myself I have sworn, declares the Lord, because you have done this thing, and have not withheld your son, your only son, indeed I will greatly bless you, and I will greatly multiply your seed as the stars of the heavens, and as the sand which is on the seashore; and your seed shall possess the gate of their enemies. And in your seed all the nations of the earth shall be blessed, because you have obeyed My voice." So Abraham returned to his young men, and they arose

and went together to Beersheba; and Abraham lived
at Beersheba. (vv. 15–19)

Lessons for Our Learning

From this wonderful story of justified and rewarded faith we can
glean at least three lessons.

First: *What you retain for yourself, God will ask you to release to
Him.* It was the late Corrie ten Boom who said, "I've learned that
we must hold everything loosely, because when I grip it tightly, it
hurts when the Father pries my fingers loose and takes it from me!"[5]
Whatever we try to keep for ourselves—whether it be our children,
parents, position, or some cherished dream for our future—God
wants us to lay that before Him, trusting Him with what is most
dear and precious to us. And He is worthy of that trust, as the next
lesson reveals.

Second: *What you release to God, He will replace with something
better.* The replacement may not always come as quickly as Abraham's
did, but it *will* come (compare Eccles. 11:1).

Third: *Whenever God replaces, He also rewards.* On this we can
rely, because rewarding is a part of God's very nature. Remember
what the writer of Hebrews tells us? "He is a rewarder of those who
seek Him" (11:6b). But He cannot reward when we will not release
and allow Him to replace. As we conclude our study, reflect on
these words from poet Martha Snell Nicholson.

> One by one He took them from me,
> All the things I valued most,
> Until I was empty-handed;
> Every glittering toy was lost,
>
> And I walked earth's highways, grieving,
> In my rags and poverty.
> Till I heard His voice inviting,
> "Lift your empty hands to Me!"
>
> So I held my hands toward Heaven,
> And He filled them with a store
> Of His own transcendent riches
> Till they could contain no more.

---

5. In a personal conversation with Chuck Swindoll.

And at last I comprehended
With my stupid mind and dull,
That God COULD not pour His riches
Into hands already full!⁶

God needs the open hands of a convert in order to manufacture a saint. Are you willing to open *your* hands to Him?

 Living Insights STUDY ONE

Undoubtedly, when Abraham offered his son, it was the most difficult trial he ever faced. The story drips with pathos wrung from an anguished father's heart.

Read through the story in Genesis 22 again, this time putting yourself in Abraham's place and one of your children on the altar. What doubts or questions come to mind?

_____

_____

_____

_____

In a word, what sustained Abraham during this crisis in his life (see Heb. 11:17–19)?

_____

_____

What role do crises play in our lives (see James 1:2–4)?

_____

_____

Romans 8:28 reveals that all things work together for good. Read verses 28–29, and make as many observations as you can about the passage.

_____

_____

6. Martha Snell Nicholson, "Treasures," in *Ivory Palaces* (Wilmington, Calif.: Martha Snell Nicholson, 1946), p. 67.

_____

_____

_____

_____

_____

Define what "good" is in verse 28.

_____

_____

🍇 *Living Insights*

In today's lesson we surveyed four crises in Abraham's life, studying the final crisis in some detail. Let's take a few minutes now to shift the focus from Abraham's life to yours.

As you survey your life, list a few of the major crises you have endured.

1. _____

2. _____

3. _____

4. _____

What is the main lesson you learned from each one?

1. _____

_____

2. _____

_____

3. _____

_____

4. _____

_____

Of those crises, which was the most difficult for you to face?

_____

Why?

_____

_____

In what ways are you more like Christ because of those crises?

_____

_____

_____

Chapter 13
BRIDLING THE BEAST IN YOUR BODY
James 3:1–12

Can you name the muscle in your body that receives more exercise and less control than any other?

Medically, they say it's only a two-ounce slab of muscle, mucous membrane, and nerves that enables us to chew, taste, swallow food, and articulate words. Redefined in nontechnical, relational terms—it's a two-ounce beast, sometimes.

Sometimes it frames deceit (Ps. 50:19), devises destruction (Ps. 52:2), devours (Ps. 52:4), is a sharp sword (Ps. 57:4), breaks bones (Prov. 25:15), backbites (Prov. 25:23), flatters (Prov. 28:23), and poisons (Rom. 3:13). You know this protean lump simply as the tongue.

It's the sometimes beastly nature of the tongue that James lashes with his pen in today's passage. And the truth of his words cuts more deeply than any other New Testament writer's. But is it our literal tongues that are the real problem? No. In Matthew 15, Jesus unmasks the culprit that controls the tongue.

> And after He called the multitude to Him, He said to them, "Hear, and understand. Not what enters into the mouth defiles the man, but what proceeds out of the mouth, this defiles the man. . . . Do you not understand that everything that goes into the mouth passes into the stomach, and is eliminated? But the things that proceed out of the mouth come from the heart, and those defile the man. For out of the heart come evil thoughts, murders, adulteries, fornications, thefts, false witness, slanders."
> (vv. 10–11, 17–19)

The tongue is neither friend nor foe. It's merely a messenger that delivers the dictates of a desperately sick heart. So every time James uses the word *tongue* in our passage today, think *heart*.

Look closely now as James peers with the Great Physician's light at the tongue and teaches us about our hearts.

Introduction

James commences his examination with a surprising command.

Command

> Let not many of you become teachers, my breth-
> ren, knowing that as such we shall incur a stricter
> judgment. (James 3:1)

Is James condemning the teaching ministry? No. Actually, he's warning against clamoring for the position without carefully weighing the cost. It is important to understand that teachers will be judged more strictly than most. Why? Because they're responsible for teaching truth—God's truth—not their own opinions. Because the words teachers sow will affect many lives. And because teachers are expected to model the truth they teach. James explained it this way.

Explanation

> For we all stumble in many ways. If anyone does not
> stumble in what he says, he is a perfect man, able
> to bridle the whole body as well. (v. 2)

This especially applies to teachers. Since no one is infallible, and since the tongue is the tool of the teaching trade, teachers must master the use of this tool to avoid stumbling into "a stricter judgment."

Clarification

Before we move deeper into our passage, let's pause to be sure we understand two important points. First, James is not condemning teaching; he's only warning against rushing into the profession without weighing the responsibility. And second, James is not promoting silence; he's proposing control.

Exposition

In verses 3–5, James emphasizes the power of the tongue through the use of three illustrations.

The Tongue: Small but Powerful

> Now if we put the bits into the horses' mouths so
> that they may obey us, we direct their entire body
> as well. (v. 3)

With a length of rope or a few strips of leather and a small piece of metal in a horse's mouth, a rider can control the horse's whole body. In the same way, James says, the tongue is a bit, a small, two-ounce bit nestled in our mouths that controls the direction of our lives.

Next, James likens the tongue to a rudder, something proportionately smaller than the bit when compared to the size of the ships it guides.

> Behold, the ships also, though they are so great and are driven by strong winds, are still directed by a very small rudder, wherever the inclination of the pilot desires. (v. 4)

Through the centuries, as ships have grown larger and heavier, James' illustration has grown more poignant than he could possibly have imagined. Yet, despite the fact that our floating behemoths could swallow whole the vessels of James' day, they still have their course determined by a comparatively small slab of metal called a rudder. The rudder of the human body is that small slab of muscle called the tongue.

Horses, ships, and now James' third and most extreme analogy, fire.

> So also the tongue is a small part of the body, and yet it boasts of great things. Behold, how great a forest is set aflame by such a small fire! (v. 5)

A tiny spark, smaller than a fingernail, holds the power to destroy thousands of acres of forest. Such is the power of the tongue. "Like fire when it is controlled, the tongue held in check is a power for great good. But out of control what havoc both can cause!"[1]

The Tongue: Necessary but Dangerous

In the next three verses, James elaborates on the image used in verse 5.

> And the tongue is a fire, the very world of iniquity; the tongue is set among our members as that which defiles the entire body, and sets on fire the course of our life, and is set on fire by hell. (v. 6)

---

1. Curtis Vaughan, *James: A Study Guide* (Grand Rapids, Mich.: Zondervan Publishing House, 1969), p. 69.

As usual, James doesn't mince his words or his metaphors! Notice the phrase "the very world of iniquity." James means that the whole world of evil finds its expression through the tongue. Boastful pride, destructive anger, cutting bitterness, flattering lust—the tongue communicates them all.

Another interesting term in verse 6 is the word for "hell." Instead of using the familiar term *Hades*, James uses *Gehenna* which was in that day an actual valley outside Jerusalem that was used as a garbage dump. All the filth of the city accumulated there, just as all the evil of our sinful hearts seems to accumulate on our tongues.

In the next two verses, James changes images.

Go to any Ringling Bros. and Barnum and Bailey Circus and you'll see the truth of what he says.

> For every species of beasts and birds, of reptiles and
> creatures of the sea, is tamed, and has been tamed
> by the human race. But no one can tame the tongue.
> (vv. 7–8a)

We know how to train seals, lions, elephants, and others—just think of Gentle Ben, Lassie, Flipper, Shamu. But there's one beast not even P. T. Barnum could tame—the tongue.

With another click of his shutter, James gives us a third and final picture.

> It is a restless evil and full of deadly poison. (v. 8b)

Our tongues are like the forked menace of a poisonous snake. With them we strike and poison those around us. Remember Hitler's words when he bared his fangs against Christianity?

> Nothing will prevent me from tearing up Christian-
> ity, root and branch . . . We are not out against a
> hundred-and-one different kinds of Christianity, but
> against Christianity itself. All people who profess
> creeds . . . are traitors to the people. Even those
> Christians who really want to serve the people . . .
> we have to suppress. I myself am a heathen to the
> core.[2]

---

2. Quoted by Spiros Zodhiates in *The Behavior of Belief* (Grand Rapids, Mich.: William B. Eerdmans Publishing Co., 1959), p. 115.

This same venomous hatred later resulted in cyclon B, the poisonous gas used to kill millions at Auschwitz, Dachau, Treblinka, and elsewhere.

The Tongue: Helpful but Inconsistent

The tongue is a powerful, dangerous beast. But remember that we said only *sometimes*. Sometimes it helps mend bones instead of breaking them; sometimes it builds people up instead of tearing them down; sometimes it brings life instead of death. In verses 9–10, James illustrates the tongue's Dr. Jekyll and Mr. Hyde tendency.

> With it we bless our Lord and Father; and with it we curse men, who have been made in the likeness of God; from the same mouth come both blessing and cursing. My brethren, these things ought not to be this way.

But they are. In his book *The Behavior of Belief*, Spiro Zodhiates tells this story.

> A large family sat around the table for breakfast one morning. As the custom was, the father returned thanks, blessing God for the food. Immediately afterward, however, as was his bad habit, he began to grumble about hard times, the poor quality of the food he was forced to eat, the way it was cooked, and much more. His little daughter interrupted him with, "Father, do you suppose God heard what you said a little while ago?" "Certainly," replied the father with the confident air of an instructor. "And did He hear what you said about the bacon and the coffee?" "Of course," the father replied but not as confidently as before. And then his little girl asked him again, "Then, Father, which did God believe?"[3]

The answer is both, because both reveal the real condition of the heart.

Next, James shows how the nature of the human heart is like nothing in nature.

> Does a fountain send out from the same opening both fresh and bitter water? Can a fig tree, my breth-

---

3. Zodhiates, *The Behavior of Belief*, pp. 119–20.

ren, produce olives, or a vine produce figs? Neither
can salt water produce fresh. (vv. 11–12)

Unlike humankind, nature is consistent. Peach trees don't produce poisonous mushrooms. Only the human heart is capable of
producing such inconsistencies.

Application

Here are three simple statements concerning the tongue to help
you remember the truths James has given us. First, the tongue *de-*
files. Remember Jesus' words in Matthew 15, that it's actually the
heart which is defiled. Second, the tongue *defies.* It defies every
attempt at human control. Third, the tongue *displays* what you
really are. Justin, one of the early church fathers, once said,

> By examining the tongue, physicians find out the
> diseases of the body; and philosophers, the diseases
> of the mind and heart.[4]

Open your mouth and stick out your tongue. Now say Ah-h-h-h.
Hmmm. Your tongue looks healthy, but what has it revealed about
your heart this past week?

 Living Insights

James 3:1–12 is replete with rich images that communicate vol-
umes about the tongue. This richness of imagery is paralleled in
the book of Proverbs. Let's look at some references there to see
what Solomon has to say about the subject. In the space provided,
describe what each metaphor means.

A fountain of life (Prov. 10:11) _____

_____

A healing agent (12:18) _____

_____

4. As quoted in *The International Dictionary of Thoughts,* comp. John P. Bradley, Leo F.
Daniels, Thomas C. Jones (Chicago, Ill.: J. G. Ferguson Publishing Co., 1969), p. 726.

A tree of life (15:4) _____

_____

Something more precious than gold and jewels (20:15) _____

_____

What image do you think comes to mind with the people you talk to? If it's not one of the above, think of an image that best describes your conversations.

_____

_____

Which problems relating to the tongue do you struggle with?

☐ Complaining   ☐ Talking crudely

☐ Bragging   ☐ Talking flippantly

☐ Lying   ☐ Talking condescendingly

☐ Gossiping   ☐ Talking too much

☐ Criticizing   ☐ Talking abrasively

With which one do you struggle most? _____

_____

What can you do to bridle that quality? _____

_____

_____

Living Insights

Today's passage tells us that just as a wild horse needs to be bridled, so does the tongue. If we're to keep our words from trampling others, we must pull back on the reins and bring them under control.

What characterizes the words of the wise?

Proverbs 11:11 _____

Proverbs 15:2 _____

Proverbs 15:7 _____

Ecclesiastes 10:12 _____

Describe an example from your life when your speech was uncommonly wise.

_____

_____

_____

What characterizes the words of the fool?

Proverbs 10:14 _____

Proverbs 11:11 _____

Proverbs 15:2 _____

Proverbs 18:6 _____

Proverbs 18:7 _____

Ecclesiastes 10:14 _____

Describe an incident when your speech was embarrassingly foolish.

_____

_____

_____

If you could relive that experience, what would you say (or not say) instead?

_____

_____

_____

Chapter 14
HOW TO MUZZLE YOUR MOUTH
Psalm 39

We have dog pounds and catchers to round up stray animals, so why not a catcher and a pound for stray words?

Imagine a razor-toothed invective being cornered by a couple of word catchers.

"Careful now, he's a mean one."

"Who would let such a thing loose?"

"Aw, somebody got riled up, I suppose, and unleashed it on somebody else."

"I'd hate to see what that somebody else feels like now."

"Shredded wheat, probably. Well, let's get this pit bull of a word off the streets. C'mon, cruel word; I've got a nice big ear for you to chew on."

Now let's say you're home and these same word catchers suddenly ring your doorbell. "Excuse me, does this word belong to you? We caught it running loose, backbiting everybody where you work. Your boss said it sounded like it was yours."

Are you missing any stray words? Did you ever wish you could take back something you said? Simon Peter did. Like that rebuke he loosed on Jesus for teaching that He would be rejected, killed, and resurrected (Mark 8:31–33). The sons of thunder, James and John, wished they had kept a few of their rumblings to themselves too. Like the time when a Samaritan village refused to receive Jesus, and the overzealous brothers asked, "Lord, do You want us to command fire to come down from heaven and consume them" (Luke 9:54)?

Looking back, Peter, James, and John regretted the junkyard words they sicced on others. And it may just be that, when they felt this remorse, they turned to a song to salve their consciences—a song like Psalm 39, written by David when he, too, was feeling remorseful about some stray words. But Psalm 39 is more than just a song about remorse; it is a record of David's attempt to control his tongue.

Introductory Issues

Before we begin our study, let's familiarize ourselves with several features of this psalm.

Superscription and Author

The superscription beneath the title of Psalm 39 would actually be verse 1 in a Hebrew Bible. "For the choir director, for Jeduthun. A Psalm of David." Written by David, it is also an inspired part of the text.

This superscription appears in only two other Psalms, 62 and 77. In all three, Jeduthun is assigned the task of interpreting the song musically. According to 1 Chronicles 16 and 25, Jeduthun came from a long line of musicians, was an accomplished musician himself, and had six sons who ministered as temple musicians. You can see why David felt confident that Jeduthun could skillfully transpose the feeling of his words into music.

Subject and Style

Typically, the subject of a psalm is revealed at the beginning. In Psalm 39, however, the subject waits for us at the end.

> "Hear my prayer, O Lord, and give ear to my cry;
> Do not be silent at my tears;
> For I am a stranger with Thee,
> A sojourner like all my fathers.
> Turn Thy gaze away from me, that I may smile
>   again,
> Before I depart and am no more." (vv. 12–13)

Obviously, David is distressed. There's an ache in his heart because something has come between him and the Lord. We don't really know the details of David's sorrow, but from the constant references to his tongue and speech throughout the rest of the psalm, it appears that he may have said some things he regretted deeply.

The style of the psalm seems to flow naturally out of the four specific techniques David tries in his quest to find a way to muzzle his mouth.

Control Techniques

Let's follow David as he begins his search.

First Approach: "I Will Handle This Alone"

"I can do it by myself." That's what all of us said to our parents as children, and it also typifies David's first approach to controlling his tongue. "I can do it by myself, Lord. I don't need any help." Fifteen times David uses the words *I* and *my* in verses 1–3, a passage full of the puffing and panting of self effort.

> I said, "I will guard my ways,
> That I may not sin with my tongue;
> I will guard my mouth as with a muzzle,
> While the wicked are in my presence."
> I was dumb and silent,
> I refrained even from good;
> And my sorrow grew worse.
> My heart was hot within me;
> While I was musing the fire burned;
> Then I spoke with my tongue."

Notice that David's self effort comes in two styles. In verse 1, the plan is simply to guard what he says. Apparently that failed, however, so in verse 2 David decides to just stop talking altogether. What was the result? His sorrow grew worse. Then in verse 3 we find that David has become like a volcano about to erupt. The thoughts and feelings he has kept stuffed down have been burning and seething till he is ready to explode.

Someone has said that there are three phases in the Christian life. First, there's the "This is wonderful" stage where everything seems easy. Then, as we begin to grow, we enter into the "Boy, this is hard" phase. Now everything seems difficult. Finally, once we have matured, our philosophy becomes "This is impossible!" Sound contradictory? It is, at least to the world's way of thinking.

You see, the world prizes an "I can do it by myself" attitude, while the mature Christian learns to prize an attitude of dependence on God. Apart from God's help, all the New Year's resolutions we make to muzzle our mouths are doomed to fail. Why? Because *I* and *me* are at the root. Remember what James said? "No one can tame the tongue" (James 3:8a). It took some time, but David finally realized this about his first technique, which then led him to his second.

Second Approach: "I Cannot Handle This Alone"

Once his first technique had utterly failed, David cried out in frustration to God, asking for some insight about himself.

111

"Lord, make me to know my end,
And what is the extent of my days,
Let me know how transient I am." (v. 4)

Verse 4 is a kind of colloquialism from David's day, which, in effect, is saying, "Lord, help me to see myself as You see me." The Greeks were only partially right when they taught that the beginning of wisdom was to "Know thyself." Real wisdom is to see ourselves through the lens of God's divine perspective.

Following his request, David then announces three things that God has shown him about himself. First, David learned that his life was brief.

"Behold, Thou hast made my days as handbreadths."
(v. 5a)

In David's day, you measured things by the cubit. Or if you wanted an even shorter measure, there was the handbreadth, literally the span from the tip of the thumb to the tip of the little finger. David realizes that his days are short.

Next, David recognizes that he is weak.

"And my lifetime as nothing in Thy sight,
Surely every man at his best is a mere breath. Selah."[1]
(v. 5b)

In the infinity of God's sight, the best that man's lifetime can be compared to is a brief puff of air, "a mere breath" that can't be held for long. David's mind is pierced with how fragile our human lives are.

Finally, God taught David that he was proud.

"Surely every man walks about as a phantom;
Surely they make an uproar for nothing;
He amasses riches, and does not know who will
gather them." (v. 6)

The word *phantom* literally means "an image." The idea is that each of us is concerned with keeping up an image that others will applaud and amassing a fortune that others will inherit. But all that anxiety and attention is ultimately futile because life here on earth is so ephemeral (see Eccles. 1–2).

---

1. Notice that David wrote "Selah" at the end of this verse and verse 11. It's a musical notation indicating a pause for emphasis or meditation.

Summing it all up, God was showing David that he wasn't supposed to even try to handle it alone. The apostle Paul records how he learned this same lesson in 2 Corinthians 12. Apparently, he was afflicted with something he called his "thorn in the flesh."

> Concerning this I entreated the Lord three times that it might depart from me. And He has said to me, "My grace is sufficient for you, for power is perfected in weakness." (vv. 8–9a)

The word *perfected* means "reaches its ultimate." God's power reaches its ultimate in us when we admit our weakness and depend on Him. How did Paul respond to this news?

> Most gladly, therefore, I will rather boast about my weaknesses, that the power of Christ may dwell in me. Therefore I am well content with weaknesses, with insults, with distresses, with persecutions, with difficulties, for Christ's sake; for when I am weak, then I am strong. (vv. 9b–10)

Know thyself? Paul did as few saints do.

Third Approach: "I Don't Want to Handle This Alone"

At this point David moves a step closer to God's plan for the believer. You can almost hear the exasperated sigh in his voice as he finally asks, "Lord, what do I do?"

> "And now, Lord, for what do I wait?
> My hope is in Thee.
> Deliver me from all my transgressions;
> Make me not the reproach of the foolish."
> (Ps. 39:7–8)

The destruction wrought by David's transgressions weighs heavily on his conscience. He feels guilty, embarrassed, ready to try the one technique God prescribes for the tongue.

Fourth Approach: "Lord, You Handle This for Me"

Listen to what happens when David leans on the Lord's strength instead of his own.

> "I have become dumb, I do not open my mouth,
> Because it is Thou who hast done it." (v. 9)

What a tremendous breakthrough! From an out-of-control rage to an obedient stillness, David finally discovers the control he has been searching for. And who gets the credit? "The Lord," David says, "He's the One who made it possible."

The sweetness of David's victory over the tongue is tinged, however, with the pain of God's ongoing chastening. So he asks that this plague, meaning God's reproofs, be removed.

> "Remove Thy plague from me;
> Because of the opposition of Thy hand, I am
>   perishing.
> With reproofs Thou dost chasten a man for
>   iniquity;
> Thou dost consume as a moth what is precious to
>   him;
> Surely every man is a mere breath. Selah."
> (vv. 10–11)

Concluding Prayer

Like all of us, David wishes he could take back some of the things he has said during his life. This psalm, however, was not one of them. David wants God to hear these words. So he prays,

> "Hear my prayer, O Lord, and give ear to my cry;
> Do not be silent at my tears;
> For I am a stranger with Thee,
> A sojourner like all my fathers.
> Turn Thy gaze away from me, that I may smile
>   again,
> Before I depart and am no more." (vv. 12–13)

Are you exhausted from trying to tame a tongue that simply refuses to be bridled? Alone, none of us can do it. But with the Lord, there's the hope of strength and a second wind.

> Those who wait for the Lord
> Will gain new strength;
> They will mount up with wings like eagles,
> They will run and not get tired,
> They will walk and not become weary. (Isa. 40:31)

In Hebrew, the term for *wait* means "to twist or stretch." It's the idea of twisting threads around one another to make a great rope that will not break. Isaiah is saying that those who twist their weaknesses around the strength of the Lord will gain new strength. And with this new strength we can keep our tongues on a leash!

 Living Insights   STUDY ONE

Psalm 39 reflects that David knew how to muzzle his mouth. He struggled, but he finally learned the importance of timing and the value of a word spoken in right circumstances. Let's explore the Scriptures further to see what they say about the tongue.

Psalm 19:14 _____

_____

Proverbs 15:23 _____

_____

Proverbs 17:27–28 _____

_____

Proverbs 25:11 _____

_____

Ecclesiastes 3:7b _____

_____

James 1:19 _____

_____

Now weave the passages together in the form of a prayer. Strive to make it specific and personal.

Dear God,

_____

_____

_____

_____

_____

_____

_____

_____

_____

_____

 Living Insights

The following verses from Proverbs speak to the issue of the tongue. Skim through as many as your time allows. As you do, circle the ones that are particularly applicable to you.

Proverbs

4:24	19:1, 5, 9, 28
5:2–4	20:15, 17, 19, 20
6:12, 14, 16–19	21:6, 23
8:6–8, 13	22:10, 11, 14, 17–21
10:11, 14, 18–21, 31–32	23:9, 16
11:9, 11, 12–13	24:1–2, 26, 28–29
12:6, 13–14	25:11–13, 14, 15, 18, 23
13:2–3	26:20–22, 23–28
14:3, 5, 23	27:2, 5, 14
15:1–2, 4, 7, 14, 26, 28	28:23
16:13, 23–24, 27–28	29:20
17:4, 10, 20, 27–28	30:5–6, 8–9
18:2, 4, 6–8, 13, 20, 21	31:26

If you need further help in controlling your tongue, pick up a copy of _You Are What You Say_ by Karen Burton Mains or _Words That Hurt, Words That Heal_ by Carole Mayhall.

Chapter 15

THE WISE, THE UNWISE, AND THE OTHERWISE

(PART ONE)

James 3:13–16

Borrowing an old woodsmen's proverb, Carl Sandburg titled the sixty-eighth chapter of his tome *Abraham Lincoln: The Prairie Years and The War Years*, "A Tree Is Best Measured when It's Down."[1] The chapter carefully measures the tall, stately life of a president who was felled by an assassin's bullet.

This woodsmen's proverb aptly describes a truth about all our lives: Only after death can we begin to measure the impact of a life. This was especially true of another leader who, like Lincoln, governed a nation and is remembered for his insightful writing—Solomon. A cross section of his life reveals that he was an author, poet, songwriter, artist, king, diplomat, theologian, teacher, zoologist, psychologist, philosopher, financier, engineer, and architect.

How could Solomon's success grow to such unparalleled heights? The answer is found in 2 Chronicles 1, beginning in verse 6.

> And Solomon went up there before the Lord to the bronze altar which was at the tent of meeting, and offered a thousand burnt offerings on it.
> In that night God appeared to Solomon and said to him, "Ask what I shall give you." (vv. 6–7)

Solomon was just beginning his reign when God suddenly made him that incredible, unconditional offer. To Solomon's credit, his first response wasn't a greedy one. Instead, he humbly praised God for His goodness, which then led to his request.

> And Solomon said to God, "Thou hast dealt with my father David with great lovingkindness, and hast made me king in his place. Now, O Lord God, Thy

---

1. Carl Sandburg, *Abraham Lincoln: The Prairie Years and The War Years*, one-volume edition (New York, N.Y.: Harcourt Brace Jovanovich, Publishers, 1982), p. 728.

promise to my father David is fulfilled; for Thou hast made me king over a people as numerous as the dust of the earth. Give me now wisdom and knowledge, that I may go out and come in before this people; for who can rule this great people of Thine?" (vv. 8–10)

Solomon asked for only two things, wisdom and knowledge. Not the theoretical kind of knowledge that could grasp abstract matters, but the ability to apply divine truth to daily life. Although Solomon was an intelligent, well-educated king, he recognized that he lacked the wisdom which only God could provide. This humility of heart greatly pleased God.

> And God said to Solomon, "Because you had this in mind, and did not ask for riches, wealth, or honor, or the life of those who hate you, nor have you even asked for long life, but you have asked for yourself wisdom and knowledge, that you may rule My people, over whom I have made you king, wisdom and knowledge have been granted to you. And I will give you riches and wealth and honor, such as none of the kings who were before you has possessed, nor those who will come after you." (vv. 11–12)

About a thousand years after Solomon's day, James wrote a letter to a group of Jews who had been driven by persecution from their homeland in Palestine. In it, he explained that trials are inevitable and that they occur for a purpose (James 1:2–4). But, in order for that purpose to be worked out in their lives, one ingredient was essential—*wisdom*. So, James counseled, follow Solomon's example and ask for it!

> But if any of you lacks wisdom, let him ask of God, who gives to all men generously and without reproach, and it will be given to him. (v. 5)

The only other time James mentions the word *wisdom* in his letter is in the third chapter, which deals, appropriately, with the tongue. It begins with a sober warning about becoming teachers, then it discusses the two basic tools all teachers use to communicate truth—the tongue (3:1–12) and their lives (v. 13). The remaining verses develop the importance of *wisdom* in the life of a teacher. Not human wisdom, mind you, but divine wisdom. The kind we all need to ask for—as Solomon did.

Test of True and False Wisdom

As is true of all valuable possessions, wisdom has its counterfeits. So, beginning in verse 13, James teaches us how to recognize the genuine article.

Divine Wisdom: Genuine

Let's look carefully at the two specific tests of someone who is wise.

> Who among you is wise and understanding? Let him show by his good behavior his deeds in the gentleness of wisdom. (v. 13)

The first test James mentions is *good behavior.* It means "to return or turn back," with the root idea being to change or return to the truth. With this phrase, James is saying that a wise person is someone whose life is changing in accordance with the truth of God's Word.

Another test of true wisdom is *gentle deeds.* Today people tend to associate the word *gentleness* with being a jellyfish—something spineless and spiritless. In James' day, however, quite the opposite was true. Then, gentleness meant bringing a high-spirited horse under control. The spirit and strength of the horse weren't lost, simply harnessed. Gentleness also referred to a brilliant teacher who could debate others without getting angry or a soothing medicine that brought comfort to a painful wound.

The qualifications for being wise have nothing to do with your I.Q. or your ability to pack away facts or your impressive eloquence. The test of wisdom is a life that is patterned after the truth and is under control.

One of the greatest problems among new Christians is the desire to hit the road running to set the world straight. Typically, the first place they run to is the home. There they declare spiritual martial law and billy-club family members with Bible verses every time one of them steps out of line. And then these new believers can't understand why their loved ones don't stand in line to enlist in the ranks and sing "Onward, Christian Soldiers." What's lacking in these new believers? *Wisdom*—balanced by the gentleness and control that Paul carefully described to his young friend Timothy.

> And the Lord's bond-servant must not be quarrelsome, but be kind to all, able to teach, patient when

wronged, with gentleness correcting those who are
in opposition. (2 Tim. 2:24–25a)

Human Wisdom: Counterfeit

In contrast to divine wisdom, which is characterized by a changed
and controlled life, James reveals the marks of human wisdom.

But if you have bitter jealousy and selfish ambition
in your heart, . . . (James 3:14a)

Did you notice the phrase, "in your heart?" These two marks,
jealousy and selfish ambition, are deeply embedded motives in the
unwise heart. People often confuse jealousy with its evil twin, envy.
What's the difference? Envy begins with empty hands and mourns
for what it does not have. Jealousy begins with full hands but is
threatened by the thought of losing what it possesses. James is
saying that an unwise person is someone who tends to be suspicious,
resistant, and given to rivalry.

The second mark—selfish ambition—is the desire to be seen,
quoted, and respected (see Matt. 23:1–7). It's the motive that
drives people to push themselves to the top. Like those teachers
Paul refers to in Philippians 1:15 and 17, who taught Christ "out
of selfish ambition rather than from pure motives." These men hun-
gered for the prominence of position, not for gentleness and good
behavior. The wise, however, allow God to open doors instead of
trying to force them open themselves.

Characteristics of False Wisdom

In the second half of verse 14, James argues for rooting out these
hidden motives, saying, in effect, "If this is down deep in your
heart, don't keep on as if it weren't! Face it, deal with it as sin,
confess it and seek wisdom." He goes on to heighten the urgency
of his request by revealing five characteristics of false wisdom.

Do not be arrogant and so lie against the truth. This
wisdom is not that which comes down from above,
but is earthly, natural, demonic. (James 3:14b–15)

Arrogant

The first of the ugly faces of false wisdom is arrogance—ration-
alizing your own sins or even boasting that the end justifies the
means, that the bad done wasn't all that bad, or that everybody

does it. In ancient times, this word was used to describe a person who boasted about winning an election dishonestly.

Unfortunately, many in the church today attempt to shelter their arrogance under the umbrella of grace. But grace doesn't excuse sin, and make no mistake about it, arrogance *is* sin (see 4:16).

Theologian Charles Hodge explained the relationship between divine grace and the human heart.

> The doctrines of grace humble man without degrading him and exalt him without inflating him.[2]

Now that's *true* wisdom.

Lying against the Truth

How do Christians justify their arrogance? By lying against the truth. The natural inclination of human wisdom is not simply to ignore or dodge the truth; it is to lie against it. The New English Bible renders this phrase, "a defiance of the truth."

When a life is out of step with Scripture, there will eventually be a manipulation of the truth to justify following a drumbeat different from God's. The result is self-deception. It's like getting the first wall up on a new home and suddenly realizing that your measurements are wrong. But instead of admitting the mistake, you design a new ruler to fit the inaccurate measurements of the first wall. The entire house ends up a crooked disaster.

Earthly

According to verse 15, false wisdom has an *earthly* origin. It views everything from a strictly horizontal perspective: earthly success, earthly standards, earthly motives, earthly attitudes, earthly methods, earthly everything!

Natural

An adequate rendering of the word *natural* is *soulish,* meaning "fleshly, not related to the Spirit of God." It denotes a wisdom whose vision is limited to things temporal, not eternal.

---

2. Spiros Zodhiates, *The Behavior of Belief* (Grand Rapids, Mich.: William B. Eerdmans Publishing Co., 1959), p. 143.

Demonic

This mindset is characteristic of demons. They are brilliant and know a great deal—even about God—but there is no change, no obedience, and no yielding of self to God.

Results of False Wisdom

In verse 16, James reminds us first of the roots of false wisdom—bitter jealousy and selfish ambition—then he identifies the fruit.

> For where jealousy and selfish ambition exist, there is disorder and every evil thing. (v. 16)

Disorder

By *disorder*, James means more than just confusion. He means disharmony, antagonism, and the absence of unity and stability. When a teaching results in rivalry, rather than building up in love, it is *not* wisdom from above.

Every Evil Thing

And when human wisdom is taught, it lifts the lid on all sorts of worthless, petty, evil things. Like Pandora's box, the human heart is home to a haunting array of sinful thoughts (Mark 7:20–23).

Conclusion

While it may be true that a tree is best measured when it's down, the fruit of a tree is best measured when it's up. Jesus said, in Matthew 12:33, that a tree is known by its fruit. What are the fruits of your life? Do people see good behavior and gentleness, or disorder and every evil thing?

By the end of Solomon's life, the royal tree that once stood so straight and tall had rotted from within. Although in the springtime of his life he had written, "The fear of the Lord is the beginning of knowledge; Fools despise wisdom and instruction" (Prov. 1:7), by the autumn of his life he had ceased fearing God and simply depended on his own human wisdom. He was no longer the world's wisest man; he had become the world's wisest fool.

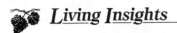

Living Insights

After reading a passage like James 3:13–18, the question for each of us to think over is, "What is my life saying to others?" Let's try to uncover some possible answers in the following study.

Do you ever struggle with jealousy? What do you think drives your emotional desire to be jealous?

_____

_____

_____

Reviewing what you learned in today's lesson, how is envy different from jealousy?

_____

_____

_____

Have the tendrils of selfish ambition taken root in your life? Describe any fruit this poisonous plant has produced.

_____

_____

_____

Jealousy and selfish ambition do not exist in some display case in a musty museum; they are on display daily in our own lives. Think about a situation where these twin destroyers wreaked their havoc through you. What led up to it, and how do you think you might have prevented it?

_____

_____

_____

Take some time now to ask your heavenly Father for His wisdom so that you may know how you can align your perspective and behavior with His.

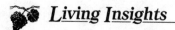

God told Solomon he could ask for anything he wanted. Sounds like a child's dream—to rub a magic lamp and get a genie who grants three wishes—doesn't it? But God is not a genie. He does, however, grant wishes to His children. But He does so purposefully, not arbitrarily. Let's examine this thought a little more by turning again to Solomon.

Read through 2 Chronicles 1:1–12.

How did God and Solomon relate to one another?

_____

_____

What do you think is God's main purpose for you?

_____

_____

What do you need to carry out His design for your life?

_____

_____

If you don't really know, pray about it. Remember, He gives wisdom to all. And He gives it generously, without reproach (James 1:5).

Chapter 16

THE WISE, THE UNWISE, AND THE OTHERWISE
(PART TWO)
James 3:17–18

F ew places are more barren or more desolate than the Libyan
Desert. Bounded on the north by the Mediterranean Sea, the
east by Egypt, the south by Chad, and the west by Algeria, this
scorched plain of sand and rocky plateaus is home to only a few
wandering nomads.

That's what makes it so incredible that an emerald Eden could
thrive in the heart of this North African desert. But one did. Miles
of green, luxuriant crops and ripening fruit swayed against the backdrop of an endless, sand-colored emptiness.

Now, in order for that garden to grow in the naturally parched
soil, a commodity very unnatural to the desert had to be piped
in—water! Through an experiment designed to test whether a desert could be a productive place, water was pumped from distant
wells into vast reservoirs. Then seeds were planted, and the trans-
formation that followed was nothing short of a miracle. That experiment proved that, if sufficient water was provided, then the desert
could produce.

Why are we starting a message on James 3 in the middle of the
Libyan Desert? Because it graphically illustrates what James teaches.
Without the Savior, our lives are like that parched, unproductive
desert. A desolation exists in our souls that ruins rather than reju-
venates. Listen as James describes the desert condition of our natural
wisdom.

> But if you have bitter jealousy and selfish ambition
> in your heart, do not be arrogant and so lie against
> the truth. This wisdom is not that which comes
> down from above, but is earthly, natural, demonic.
> For where jealousy and selfish ambition exist, there
> is disorder and every evil thing. (James 3:14–16)

Now, in order for divine wisdom to take root in our lives, something very unnatural to our hearts must be piped in by faith—the

living water of the Savior (John 7:38). Under the Holy Spirit's supervision, our lives can blossom with a divine wisdom we could never produce on our own.

Tests of True Wisdom

In our last lesson, we learned that the tests of true wisdom are good behavior and gentleness (James 3:13). In a word, good behavior means *change:* an inner willingness to obey God's Word. Gentleness refers to strength under *control,* like that seen in a high-spirited horse that has been well trained.

Characteristics of Divine Wisdom

When these two divinely encoded seeds—good behavior and gentleness—are sown, they produce a totally unnatural, even supernatural crop. You won't find any of it at your local grocery store, but you can see at least seven fruits of divine wisdom on display in our passage today.

> But the wisdom from above is first pure, then peaceable, gentle, reasonable, full of mercy and good fruits, unwavering, without hypocrisy. (James 3:17)

Let's take some time to inspect each of these fruits.

Pure

"But the wisdom from above is first pure." The word *first* not only means first in a list, but first in importance. The primary fruit of divine wisdom is purity. The word means "freedom from defilement, without contamination, clean." It suggests not only moral cleanliness, but also purity of motive—the same kind Peter refers to in his admonition to wives of unbelieving husbands.

> In the same way, you wives, be submissive to your own husbands so that even if any of them are disobedient to the word, they may be won without a word by the behavior of their wives, as they observe your chaste and respectful behavior. (1 Pet. 3:1–2)

When someone drifts in their obedience to Christ, often our first reaction is to wag our fingers and cluck our tongues. But Peter says to bring them back to Christ through our chaste, loving, and respectful behavior. The term for *chaste* refers to the same inner purity of motive that James speaks of.

Purity also carries with it a peculiar promise. Jesus said, "Blessed are the pure in heart, for they shall see God" (Matt. 5:8). But the Bible also teaches that no man has seen God (John 1:18). Then what did Jesus mean? He meant that the pure in heart will know God so intimately that they will see Him come to their rescue when tempted or come alongside as their closest friend when facing trials. Purity clears our vision to see Him at work in everything we do.

Peaceable

Notice the difference between the divine fruit of peace and the natural products of human wisdom, which are listed in verse 14: bitter jealousy, selfish ambition, arrogance, and lying. Clearly, we are prone to quarrel by nature. But when wisdom from above fills our hearts, a peaceable nature blossoms, one that helps heal relationships rather than tear them apart.

Now some may say, "Well, I'm not by nature a calm and peaceable person." That's the whole point. None of us are peaceful by nature. Remember, we are like the desert. But when God's wisdom rains gently upon that desert, a peaceable attitude springs to life.

Gentle

The Greek term for gentle in verse 17, epieikes, is different from the term James used four verses earlier. This new term is extremely hard to explain, because it means more than any one English word can convey. Some have rendered it "equitable, fair, or moderate." "Tolerant" would be better, but even it falls short. Perhaps William Barclay captured the meaning best when he said,

> The man who is epieikes is the man who knows when it is actually wrong to apply the strict letter of the law. He knows how to forgive when strict justice gives him a perfect right to condemn. He knows how to make allowances, when not to stand upon his rights, how to temper justice with mercy, always remembers that there are greater things in the world than rules and regulations. . . . Matthew Arnold called it "sweet reasonableness" and it is the ability to extend to others the kindly consideration we would wish to receive ourselves.[1]

1. William Barclay, The Letters of James and Peter, rev. ed., The Daily Study Bible series (Philadelphia, Pa.: Westminster Press, 1976), pp. 95–96.

Reasonable

As you might suspect from Matthew Arnold's description of what *gentle* means, there's a close connection between it and the next characteristic, being *reasonable*. Like two corresponding pieces of a puzzle, gentleness and reasonableness fit snugly together because of their subtle differences. The word *gentle* is really written for those in places of authority over others. *Reasonable*, on the other hand, is especially fitting for those who are under someone else's authority.

The original term comes from two Greek words that combine to mean "easily persuaded." It's the opposite of being stubborn and obstinate. This quality is reflected by those who are open, conciliatory, and easy to work with.

A classic example of someone who acted reasonably is recorded in Genesis 13. It's the story of how Abraham (still called Abram at this point in his life) settled a prosperity problem that arose with his nephew Lot.

> Now Abram was very rich in livestock, in silver and in gold. . . . Now Lot, who went with Abram, also had flocks and herds and tents. And the land could not sustain them while dwelling together; for their possessions were so great that they were not able to remain together. (vv. 2, 5–6)

Notice how Abraham, the older of the two, took the initiative to create a compromise.

> Then Abram said to Lot, "Please let there be no strife between you and me, nor between my herdsmen and your herdsmen, for we are brothers. Is not the whole land before you? Please separate from me: if to the left, then I will go to the right; or if to the right, then I will go to the left." (vv. 8–9)

Now that's reasonable! Are you that kind of person? Can you give serious thought to an opinion that differs from yours without feeling threatened or getting angry?

Full of Mercy and Good Fruits

The natural wisdom we inherit from our sin nature infuses us with cynicism and harshness, especially toward the sufferings of others. The wisdom that comes down from above, however, reacts to suffering with mercy and good fruits. Mercy is a compassionate *attitude,* and good fruits are *actions* that naturally flow from mercy.

In the first century, the word *mercy* was commonly used to describe people's feelings toward someone who had suffered unjustly. In the New Testament, however, this same word is used several times to describe the attitude a believer should have toward those who suffer due to problems they have caused themselves.

Surprised? Anyone can feel for people who suffer through no fault of their own, but God's mercy enables us to have pity and compassion for those who have caused their own sorrow. This divine mercy then issues forth into practical help: "good fruits." William Barclay wrote, "We can never say that we have truly pitied anyone until we have helped him."[2]

Unwavering

The original term for *unwavering* means "a person of fixed principles." Unwavering believers faithfully adhere to the principles in God's Word regardless of the circumstances. Though others may say, "When in Rome, do as the Romans do," this individual lives under the precept, "When in Rome, do as the believer should do."

Coupled with an unwavering fidelity to truth, this individual is decisive, one who is not afraid to make decisions based on Scripture.

Without Hypocrisy

Our modern word *hypocrisy* comes from the first-century term *hupokrites,* used to describe a person who was an actor. In Greek theater, actors normally played several parts by simply wearing a different mask for each character. Today when we use the word *hypocrite* we mean anyone who wears masks, who pretends to be someone he or she is not.

True wisdom is never two-faced or deceptive. It is completely and simply honest.

The Result of True Wisdom

Now that we've completed our fruit inspection, let's step back and see what result divine wisdom can make in our lives.

2. Barclay, *Letters of James and Peter,* p. 97.

And the seed whose fruit is righteousness is sown in
peace by those who make peace. (James 3:18)

To understand this highly compressed sentence, you must remember that, in James, peace means being rightly related to one
another. It's not a vertical peace between God and man; it's a
horizontal peace between human beings. Those who disturb this
peace between themselves and others will not enjoy a righteous
lifestyle before God.

Nothing is more barren and desolate than the Libyan Desert—
except the human heart apart from God. But as rain gives life to
the desert, so can God cultivate a garden of divine wisdom in us
through the living water of His Holy Spirit. Are you ready to shift
from being a fruit inspector to a fruit grower? Take a moment now
to begin watering the seeds of His wisdom with this prayer from
St. Francis of Assisi.

Lord, make me an instrument of Your peace!
Where there is hatred, let me sow love;
Where there is injury, pardon;
Where there is doubt, faith;
Where there is despair, hope;
Where there is darkness, light;
Where there is sadness, joy.

O Divine Master, grant that I may not so much
   seek
To be consoled, as to console;
To be understood, as to understand;
To be loved as to love.

For it is in giving that we receive;
It is in pardoning that we are pardoned;
It is in dying that we are born to eternal life.[3]

3. St. Francis of Assisi, as quoted by Spiros Zodhiates in The Behavior of Belief (Grand
Rapids, Mich.: William B. Eerdmans Publishing Co., 1959), pp. 181–82.

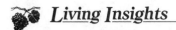 *Living Insights*

James 3:13 names two "seed" traits called *good behavior* and *gentle deeds*. Each trait reveals a willingness to change the quality of one's life. Measure your willingness to change and exercise control in your life by examining verses 17–18.

Wisdom is *first* pure, free from defilement and contamination. Try contemplating on two vital areas of your life: morality and motives. If either of these areas concerns you, you may find help in one of these books:

Moral purity. John White's *Eros Defiled: The Christian and Sexual Sin* (Downers Grove, Ill.: InterVarsity Press, 1977).

Clean motives. Larry Crabb's *Inside Out* (Colorado Springs, Colo.: NavPress, 1988).

Joseph was a person who exercised godly control over his morals and motives. Read his story in Genesis 37 and 39–50. Note three things that encourage you to keep pure morals and motives.

Wisdom is also peaceable, that is, it seeks to bring people together, not to polarize them. Thumb through your mental concordance and name a person who acted as a peacemaker. What steps did he or she take to achieve peace?

What is the downside risk of becoming a peacemaker (see Matt. 5:9–12)?

Wisdom is gentle, equitable, and tolerant. Parents, church leaders, and all who oversee others have daily opportunities to display godly wisdom. Think about how you treat those under your care.

131

What principles do you find in 1 Peter 5:1–3 that could help you improve your approach?

_____

_____

_____

_____

🍇 _Living Insights_

Continuing our study of James 3:17–18, we want to hold these verses up to the light again to be sure we catch every facet of this dazzling jewel called divine wisdom.

Wisdom is reasonable, easily persuaded. If you are under someone's authority, whether in the family or at work, are you cooperative or are you impervious to persuasion? Have you come to terms with the place of authority and how to work wisely under those who lead you? How does 1 Peter 2:13–17 contribute to your thinking (compare Rom. 13:1–7)?

_____

_____

_____

Wisdom is full of mercy and good fruits. If your eyes are sensitized, you cannot help but see incredible suffering around you. Mercy is exercised when compassion for an individual so grips you that you reach out to offer help. Read James 2:15–16 and Matthew 5:7. Meditate on these verses. Now, name several good fruits that come to mind from some act of mercy you have performed.

_____

_____

_____

Wisdom is unwavering, dependable, and consistent (James 1:6). Joshua and Caleb exhibited such wisdom. Read Numbers 13:17–33 and 14:1–45. Now compare 14:24 with Joshua 14:1–14. What outstanding trait did Caleb and Joshua exhibit?

_____

Wisdom is not hypocritical, does not put on a false face. Two-faced living reveals a shallow walk. Rephrase the remedy found in Romans 12:9.

_____

_____

Chapter 17

HOW FIGHTS ARE
STARTED AND STOPPED
James 4:1–10

Did you ever have to eat grass when you were growing up? In my neighborhood, that was the standard punishment for anyone who lost a fight. Victor and spectators jeered and howled while the vanquished grazed. Then we would all go play again . . . until the next fight. Fighting, playing, eating a little Saint Augustine, that's just how it was—and how it still is. Oh, we may not eat grass anymore or play as much, but we still love to fight.

Franklin Roosevelt once said, "There is nothing I love as much as a good fight."[1] Fighting is something that comes to us naturally. Why? Because we're each born with a scrappy nature that prefers going for the jugular to giving in.

The fact that we have a pugnacious nature is not a new problem either. Beginning in a field with Cain and Abel, human history is more easily traced by the bloody path of its fights than by its accomplishments. That path, sad to say, also cuts right through the church. Denominations bomb one another in Ireland, seminaries clash over doctrines, authors attack other authors in print, and on it goes, right down to the squabbles of individual saints.

It isn't surprising, then, that James addresses the problem of conflicts among Christians. Fighting, worshiping, fighting some more —it was the same two thousand years ago as it is today.

Let's listen as James jumps into the fray with some hard-hitting advice about how fights are started and stopped.

Initial Facts

The break between chapters 3 and 4 is an unfortunate one, since James neither changes the subject nor shifts his emphasis. In fact, his comments regarding the destructive nature of the tongue,

---

1. Franklin D. Roosevelt, as quoted in *Bartlett's Familiar Quotations*, 15th ed., rev. and enl., ed. Emily Morison Beck (Boston, Mass.: Little, Brown and Co., 1980), p. 779.

134

which started in chapter 3, build to a crescendo in the fourth chapter, beginning with the rhetorical question,

> What is the source of quarrels and conflicts among
> you? (4:1a)

Before we look at James' answer to this question, let's establish who "among you" refers to. If you'll look back to 3:1 and ahead to 4:11, you'll see that everything between these two verses is directed toward Christians.

Notice also how James describes the fighting by using two words that form one unit. In Greek, *quarrels* is the general term for an entire war, and *conflicts* refers more to individual battles.

Like a parent stepping into the middle of a sibling squabble, James asks his readers, "What started all this?" But before any finger pointing can start, James points his finger at the first of two root causes.

Analysis of the Problem

To expose the first root cause, James answers his first rhetorical question with a second.

First Cause: Inner Desire

> Is not the source your pleasures that wage war in
> your members? (4:1b)

The Greek term for *pleasures* means "desire or passion." It's a neutral term that, depending on the context, can refer either to evil or good desires. When our desires go unmet, however, our frustration mounts and eventually erupts into conflict. So we wage war, intent on fighting until we get our way.

Next, James mentions three specific effects of this unchecked, combative desire.

> You lust and do not have; so you commit murder.
> And you are envious and cannot obtain; so you fight
> and quarrel. You do not have because you do not
> ask. (v. 2)

Certainly most of us are not guilty of murder in a literal sense, but we do kill with our thoughts. We allow ourselves to calculate ways to assassinate someone else's character. "But at least it doesn't go any further than that," some may rationalize. Oh yes it does.

Those same murderous thoughts spur us on to the second effect James mentions, fights and quarrels—wounding with words.

The third effect is failure to pray. Why? Because we're too busy fighting. We prefer to slug things out rather than surrender the situation to God.

James not only analyzes the problem of fighting, he also anticipates a fighter's response. Such is the case in verse 3. The apostle envisioned people protesting, "But we did ask God, and He didn't answer our prayers," to which James replies,

> You ask and do not receive, because you ask with wrong motives, so that you may spend it on your pleasures. (v. 3)

Commentator Curtis Vaughan explains,

> Their requests were legitimate, but the reason for making them was illegitimate. They wanted only to satisfy their own cravings, pamper their own passions. God's glory, God's service, consideration for other people—none of these things entered into their thinking. Such prayers are an insult to God.[2]

Prayer—real prayer—allows God to come to our rescue *His* way.

Second Cause: "Kosmos" Motivation

Another cause for quarrels among believers is found in verse 4.

> You adulteresses, do you not know that friendship with the world is hostility toward God? Therefore whoever wishes to be a friend of the world makes himself an enemy of God. (v. 4)

In the New Testament, the Greek term for "world," *kosmos*, is ordinarily used to mean "the world apart from God." It signifies a self-centered, Satan-controlled philosophy that is hostile toward God. Believers war when they attempt to satisfy their inner desires by worldly motivation. Kosmos motivation means handling conflicts by fighting, pushing, and demanding until you get exactly what you want, when you want it. It's saying, "Lord, Your way is

---

2. Curtis Vaughan, *James: A Study Guide* (Grand Rapids, Mich.: Zondervan Publishing House, 1969), p. 85.

not the best way for me. I know what's best, and I will satisfy my needs by doing it the world's way instead of Yours."

What does kosmos motivation result in? First, it creates hostility toward God. Deliberately living according to the world's standards rather than God's is an act of rebellion. The second effect James mentions is enmity against God. Commentator Donald W. Burdick writes,

> To have a warm, familiar attitude toward this evil world is to be on good terms with God's enemy. It is to adopt the world's set of values and want what the world wants instead of choosing according to divine standards. The person who deliberately "chooses . . . to be a friend of the world" by that choice "becomes an enemy of God."[3]

Let's pause for a moment and consider some specific examples of what James is talking about. If you are a gifted person with leadership capabilities not being used, you may have a tendency to be impatient and manipulate circumstances to push yourself to the front. God says, "Wait, let Me open the doors. Take advantage of this time away from the limelight to deepen your trust in Me."

If you are single and eager to be married, you may be tempted to panic and hurry into a marriage relationship. But God's advice would be, "Don't run ahead of Me, I know your desires. Lean on Me and I'll help you find the right mate."

Or perhaps you've worked hard and done a good job, but somebody else received the credit. The world says that you should fight for your rights! Promote yourself, because if you don't, nobody else will. But God's viewpoint runs, "There's no need to clamor for recognition. You're here to do your work for My glory, not yours. I have seen the good that you have done and I will reward you."

See how easily our inner desires can become frustrated and how quickly our life's goal can shift from pleasing God to fighting for ourselves?

Synopsis of the Solution

Having diagnosed the causes and effects of our fighting, James next turns our attention to God's solution.

---

3. Donald W. Burdick, "James," in *The Expositor's Bible Commentary* (Grand Rapids, Mich.: Zondervan Publishing House, Regency Reference Library, 1981), vol. 12, p. 193.

The Power

> Or do you think that the Scripture speaks to no
> purpose: "He jealously desires the Spirit which He
> has made to dwell in us"? (v. 5)

The first part of the solution is the power of the Holy Spirit.
God has given us His Spirit because He jealously desires, as one
commentator put it, "the entire devotion of the heart."[4]

> God claims us entirely for Himself. No alien rela-
> tionship, such as friendship with the world, will be
> tolerated by Him. He wants the undivided devotion
> of every human heart.[5]

When believers divide their allegiance between the Lord and
the world, they end up fighting. But when we draw upon the power
of His Holy Spirit and say, "Lord, it's Your battle, please take control," the fighting subsides.

The Principle

The second part of God's solution is found in verse 6:

> But He gives a greater grace. Therefore it says, "God
> is opposed to the proud, but gives grace to the hum-
> ble." (v. 6)

Greater grace is the principle. God is saying, "I'll give abundant
grace to those who are willing to humble themselves and wait. Trust
Me and draw your strength from Me."

Practical Advice

James closes with some seasoned practical advice. Notice how
he uses the word *humble* to bracket verses 7–9. In verse 6 we're told
that God gives greater grace to the humble, and in verse 10 we're
reminded again to humble ourselves. What comes between is a
series of commands that describes the process of becoming humble
in God's sight.

> Submit therefore to God. Resist the devil and he will
> flee from you. Draw near to God and He will draw

---

4. J. B. Mayor, as quoted by Vaughan in *James: A Study Guide*, p. 88.

5. Vaughan, *James: A Study Guide*, p. 88.

near to you. Cleanse your hands, you sinners; and
purify your hearts, you double-minded. (vv. 7–8)

First, *Submit to God.* We are to cease fighting and surrender our
wills to His control. Second, *Resist the devil.* We are to resist the
promptings of the god of this world that tell us to assert ourselves;
this often leads to conflict. Third, *Draw near to God.* We are to
stay close to God by developing a loving companionship. Fourth,
Cleanse hands and purify hearts. We are to cleanse ourselves from
any moral defilement that may have created enmity between ourselves and others or God.

In verse 9, we see James' earnestness as he appeals for godly sorrow, the intense kind that grows out of a deep awareness of our sin.

Be miserable and mourn and weep; let your laughter
be turned into mourning, and your joy to gloom. (v. 9)

Finally, James sums up his advice on how fights are stopped.

Humble yourselves in the presence of the Lord, and
He will exalt you. (v. 10)

Humble yourselves. Say "uncle" to the Spirit's promptings and
surrender to God, letting Him do your fighting.

If you live your life fighting, you'll end up on the ground, and
over a lifetime, you'll end up eating a lot of grass. Wouldn't you
prefer surrendering to the One who promises to lift you up? Which
will it be: a mouthful of grass or a life full of grace?

 Living Insights   STUDY ONE

We can mow a yard full of weeds down to the ground, but unless
we pull them up by the roots, they'll just grow back again. Our
conflicts with other Christians are a lot like that. We can clip short
our malicious words whenever they surface, but unless we get to
the source, these same conflicts will just keep cropping up.

According to James 4:1, what is the general source of our conflicts?

_____

From verses 2–3, what are some of the specific causes and effects of conflict? Write your answers on the following page.

Cause	Effect
_____	_____
_____	_____
_____	_____
_____	_____

Which of these four categories do you struggle with most?

_____

What can you do to take that problem by the root and pull it out of your life?

_____

_____

_____

Living Insights   STUDY TWO

Humility is the mother of all virtue. Every good quality in a person's life is conceived within the womb of that one quality. Read through the following Scriptures and jot down what they have to say about humility.

Job 5:11 _____

Psalm 138:6 _____

Proverbs 15:33 _____

Proverbs 16:19 _____

Micah 6:8 _____

Matthew 18:4 _____

Luke 14:11 _____

One impediment to becoming a humble person is the "pride of life" (1 John 2:16), which comes from an unhealthy love for the world. In a terse, prescriptive manner, James 4:7–10 gives us the steps to breaking off our adulterous love affair with the world. Many of the commands in these verses have consequences attached to them. List the commands in the first column, and if they have results, list those in the second.

James 4:7–10

Command	Result
1. _____	_____
2. _____	_____
3. _____	_____
4. _____	_____
5. _____	_____
6. _____	_____
7. _____	_____
8. _____	_____
9. _____	_____
10. _____	_____

How was the principle in James 4:10 illustrated by Jesus' life (see Phil. 2:5–11)?

_____

_____

How could it be illustrated in your life (see Phil. 2:3–4)?

_____

_____

Chapter 18

WHEN IS IT RIGHT TO FIGHT?

Selected Scripture

In our last lesson, we looked at when it's not right to fight. Today we want to examine the flip side of that issue and ask, When *is* it right to fight—especially as Christians?

To get us thinking about this question, let's observe the action in three different arenas.

In the first arena stands a ten-year-old boy—let's make him *your* son just to keep things interesting. He's been playing happily at the park all Saturday morning; but just as he's about to bike home for lunch, three bullies kick over his bike, steal his ball, and start pounding on him. What would you have him do? Fight back, or drop to his knees and fervently start to pray?

In the next arena you are an American citizen of Arab descent, who has been drafted to fight for the United States Armed Forces. During your training, war breaks out—with the U.S. coming to Israel's side against your country of origin, which, by the way, is where most of your family is still living. What should you do? Follow your government's orders, or follow your own convictions?

Finally, in the third arena, you are a Christian student in a public school, where you desire to make Christ known. So you begin to share your faith with several classmates. The administration is made up of unbelievers, however, and they aren't too keen on your "proselytizing." In fact, they officially decide that there will be no more speaking about Christ on campus at all. Do you challenge this decision, or do you meekly obey orders?

These are tough questions in tough arenas. And being a Christian only compounds these problems, because it puts us under two authorities—the heavenly and the earthly (compare Mark 12:17). For our purposes today, we are going to listen to our heavenly Authority's instructions, putting aside popular opinion, parental training, natural logic, and American culture. So have your Bible ready, and let's see when God says it is right for a Christian to fight.

Illustrations from the Scriptures

It may surprise you to learn that the words *fight, fighting, war, warfare,* and other related terms appear nearly six hundred times in the Bible. God has much to say about this significant subject, both in the Old Testament and the New.

Old Testament

The first passage we'll look at comes from the pen of Solomon.

> There is an appointed time for everything. And there
> is a time for every event under heaven. . . .
> A time to kill, and a time to heal;
> A time to tear down, and a time to build up. . . .
> A time to love, and a time to hate;
> A time for war, and a time for peace.
> (Eccles. 3:1, 3, 8)

This passage is a familiar one, but have you ever really considered these particular verses? They are actually saying that there *are* times for warfare, fighting, and killing. Does this surprise you, perhaps going against the deeply ingrained manifesto: Thou shalt not kill?

Let's stop and give attention to this apparent contradiction. Back in Exodus 20:13, take a look at what this sixth commandment actually says,

> "You shall not *murder.* " (emphasis added)

The Hebrew root for "murder" here is *ratsach,* which often suggests premeditated murder. This command shows that God wants life preserved, not willfully destroyed in an act of hatred. And He emphasizes this in the penalty He requires for the one who murders:

> "He who strikes a man so that he dies shall surely
> be put to death." (Exod. 21:12)

Now if God prohibited all forms of killing, He certainly would not have made capital punishment—killing another person—the penalty for this crime.

Another case of biblical support for fighting and warfare is found in 1 Chronicles 5.

> The sons of Reuben and the Gadites and the
> half-tribe of Manasseh, consisting of valiant men,

men who bore shield and sword and shot with bow, and were skillful in battle . . . made war against the Hagrites, Jetur, Naphish, and Nodab. And they were helped against them, and the Hagrites and all who were with them were given into their hand; for they cried out to God in the battle, and He was entreated for them, because they trusted in Him. And . . . many fell slain, because *the war was of God.* (vv. 18–22a, emphasis added)

This may be a shocking scenario for some, but those who know their Bibles also know that God has a place for war in His sovereign plan. In fact, all through the Old Testament God blessed those righteous men and women who withstood His enemies and fought for just causes.[1]

One such righteous man was Daniel. Captured and taken to Babylon as a teen, the devout Daniel, as well as his three friends, soon found themselves under the authority of a godless king (Dan. 1). Matters came to a head when this king, the egotistical Nebuchadnezzar, built a huge image of gold and demanded that everyone in the kingdom bow down to worship it . . . or be burned to death. Daniel's friends, however, were not about to bow down to anyone other than Almighty God; and though they were cast into the fire, God blessed their resistance by keeping them from being burned—their clothes didn't even smell of smoke (chap. 3).

Daniel was put to the test in chapter 6, when he quietly defied another of the king's edicts, which prohibited prayer. For that he was cast into a den of lions, but God also blessed his resistance and kept the lions from harming him.

From these Old Testament examples we can see that God sets aside certain times for war, that He authorizes killing in certain circumstances, and that He blesses our recognition of His ultimate authority.

But, you may be thinking, that was in Old Testament times; now we're under a New Covenant. Fair enough. Let's take a look at what the New Testament has to say on this issue.

---

1. The book of Joshua, for instance, is primarily a record of conflict. And the book of Judges opens with the Israelites engaging the Canaanites in battle, attempting to drive the heathen nation out of the Promised Land. For specific battles that God blessed, think of Samson and the Philistines (Judg. 14–16), David and Goliath (1 Sam. 17), and Elijah and the prophets of Baal (1 Kings 18).

Over in Matthew 22, we find the Lord Jesus in a confrontation with the established religious leaders of the day, the Pharisees.

> Then the Pharisees went and counseled together how they might trap Him in what He said. And they sent their disciples to Him . . . saying, "Teacher, we know that You are truthful and teach the way of God in truth, and defer to no one; for You are not partial to any. Tell us therefore, what do You think? Is it lawful to give a poll-tax to Caesar, or not?" But Jesus perceived their malice, and said, "Why are you testing Me, you hypocrites? Show Me the coin used for the poll-tax." And they brought Him a denarius. And He said to them, "Whose likeness and inscription is this?" They said to Him, "Caesar's." Then He said to them, "Then render to Caesar the things that are Caesar's; and to God the things that are God's." (vv. 15–21).

A couple of things leap off the page of this passage. First, look at the strong rebuke Jesus gave them: "you hypocrites." Did this come out of the mouth of "gentle Jesus, meek and mild"? It certainly did! Jesus was not a spiritual doormat for the world to walk on. He had the courage and honesty to call things what they were.

The second thing that stands out is His concluding point in verse 21. We could paraphrase His last statement as, "You have a responsibility to the law of the land, but you also have a responsibility to the law of God." And though Jesus encouraged loyalty to Caesar, His steadfast obedience to His Father's principles sometimes put Him in the position of criticizing the evils in government.

Some examples of this criticism are His linking of tax-gatherers with harlots (Matt. 21:31); the seven long woes He leveled against the Pharisees and the abuse of their power (chap. 23); His labeling Herod "that fox"—a rather pointed remark about that leader's deceptive and wily character (Luke 13:32); and His withering condemnation of the practices of lawyers (Luke 11:45–52). But it's important to note that, in all of these instances, Jesus was fighting the evils in government, not government itself.[2]

2. Jesus' response to Pilate's interrogation in John 18 supports this idea. Pilate had been asking Jesus about His kingdom—at the back of his mind probably wondering if He was

Another New Testament example that supports fighting is the apostles' refusal to place the commands of men above those of God. The action takes place in Acts 4, where Peter and John face strong opposition from the priests and elders after having healed a lame beggar (chap. 3).

> The council . . . began to confer with one another, saying, "What shall we do with these men? For the fact that a noteworthy miracle has taken place through them is apparent to all who live in Jerusalem, and we cannot deny it. But in order that it may not spread any further among the people, let us warn them to speak no more to any man in this name." And when they had summoned them, they commanded them not to speak or teach at all in the name of Jesus. (4:15b–18)

Peter and John's response?

> "Whether it is right in the sight of God to give heed to you rather than to God, you be the judge; for we cannot stop speaking what we have seen and heard." (vv. 19–20)

So despite continued hostility, flogging, and imprisonment, the apostles never did stop speaking about what they had seen and heard; instead, they continued to serve their higher Authority (see also Acts 5:12–42).

Suggestions for Today

Let's spend a little time now translating these historical lessons into the language of today.

---

plotting to overthrow the Roman government. But listen to Jesus' answer: "My kingdom is not of this world. If My kingdom were of this world, then My servants would be fighting, that I might not be delivered up to the Jews; but as it is, My kingdom is not of this realm" (v. 36). With that phrase, "My servants would be fighting," He was saying, in effect, that if He were building a kingdom for Himself in the Roman world, He would have His men armed and fighting. But His kingdom is not there; His calling and cause are higher than the fleeting majesty of the Roman Empire. So Pilate's fears of treason were abated, and he concludes, "I find no guilt in Him" (v. 38b). Jesus did not come to overthrow governments, just the evil that so often pollutes them.

In the Personal Realm

We opened this lesson with your little ten-year-old boy getting mugged by three bullies. So our first realm of application centers around the issue of self-defense.

Often, the idea of defending yourself gets slapped down by those who backhand you with Jesus' words in Matthew 5:38–41, the familiar passage about turning the other cheek. But is it wise to use this passage to oppose teaching children to defend themselves? Is it right to expect God to honor an individual for standing there and being beaten to a pulp? The psalmist would say no.

Look at the cause of David's praise in Psalm 144.

> Blessed be the Lord, my rock,
> Who trains my hands for war,
> And my fingers for battle. (v. 1)

And in Psalm 18.

> He trains my hands for battle,
> So that my arms can bend a bow of bronze. . . .
> I pursued my enemies and overtook them,
> And I did not turn back until they were consumed.
> I shattered them, so that they were not able to rise;
> They fell under my feet. (vv. 34, 37–38)

David is not picking a fight in these passages; he is merely defending himself . . . standing up for what's right. He does not take the battering of the Holy Spirit's temple sitting down. And we shouldn't, either. After all, we aren't passive about locking our doors and protecting our possessions. So how can we do any less regarding our lives?

In the Civil Realm

From Daniel's example we can see that the government has full authority until it moves into the spiritual realm. This answers the question about military service that we posed at the start. If you are a citizen of a country—no matter your national descent—you are to defend the country of which you are a citizen (compare Rom. 13:1–7).[3]

---

3. The idea of conscientious objection is difficult to support in Scripture. One passage that addresses the topic is Deuteronomy 20:3–8.

In the Spiritual Realm

Jesus and the apostles are our models in this realm, showing us that when government moves into an area it has no right to, we are to follow God instead. And when we disobey, we are not to conduct ourselves obnoxiously but with dignity and honor, as Peter says:

> Beloved, I urge you as aliens and strangers. . . .
> Keep your behavior excellent among the Gentiles, so that in the thing in which they slander you as evildoers, they may on account of your good deeds, as they observe them, glorify God in the day of visitation. . . . Act as free men, and do not use your freedom as a covering for evil, but use it as bond-slaves of God. Honor all men; love the brotherhood, fear God, honor the king. (1 Pet. 2:11–12, 16–17)

Exhortations to Remember

After a lesson like today's there are at least two important truths we must keep in mind. First, *there is a great difference between standing for the right and having a fighting attitude.* When Paul listed the qualities an officer in the church must have, he stated that this person must not be "pugnacious, but gentle, uncontentious" (1 Tim. 3:3).

The second truth is that *there is no guarantee of safety or divine deliverance when you fight for the right.* For every Daniel who comes through resistance unscathed, there are countless thousands who suffer undeservedly for doing what's right. The crimson streams that run through Hebrews 11 are evidence enough of that.

One final note: we must exercise balance and discernment when it comes to fighting. It should never be our first course, only our last—when everything else has been tried. When there's a question of right, however, then that issue supersedes all others.

 Living Insights STUDY ONE

In Matthew 5:38–42, Jesus illustrates what our role should be when we are receiving the brunt of another person's aggression. Let's take some time now to dig a little deeper into this passage.

When Jesus says, "But I say to you" (v. 39), He contrasts verse 38 with verses 39–42. What is the issue in verse 38?

Now, what is the concern in verses 39–42?

_____

_____

Name some situations where you believe self-defense is justified.

_____

_____

How do you support your view scripturally?

_____

_____

_____

Read a commentary on this passage, and jot down any new insights you gain.

_____

_____

_____

_____

_____

_____

🍇 *Living Insights* _____ STUDY TWO

Romans 13:1–7 punctuates a believer's civil obligations while 1 Peter 2:11–17 marks out a believer's behavior before other people. List three points from each passage that impress you.

Romans 13:1–7	1 Peter 2:11–17
1. _____	1. _____
2. _____	2. _____
3. _____	3. _____

Now read Acts 4:15–21, 5:40–42, and Daniel 6. Are the apostles' actions different in principle from Daniel's? Explain any similarities or differences you observe between the two.

Similarities: _____

_____

_____

_____

Differences: _____

_____

_____

_____

Finally, based upon your conclusions, when do you think it is right to fight?

_____

_____

_____

Chapter 19
THE PERIL
OF PLAYING GOD
James 4:11–17

Years ago Eric Berne wrote a best-seller titled *Games People Play*. In it he exposed the subtle ways people manipulate others without their even being aware of what's happening. Three years after this book was published, another one, *Games Christians Play*, came out, taking readers behind the scenes in the Christian community to reveal the games played beneath a religious veneer.

For example, have you ever encountered the "When you have been a Christian as long as I have . . ." type of person? These players either were born in a choir loft or saved at age two. Their favorite ploy, making sure everyone knows that they know everything, is the well-placed put-down.

To illustrate, let's say you're an excited new Christian, and you share with one of these smug pillars of the faith that you just discovered the book of Habakkuk. This is the typical put-you-in-your-place response you can expect: "Oh, so you're just *now* getting into Habakkuk? Well, you'll just love it when you discover the Chaldean taunt-songs in chapter 2. Why, I remember studying that years ago when I was a missionary living with a migrant family. Of course, when you've been a Christian as long as I have . . ."

Another game believers love to play is: "I'd love to, but . . ." Imagine that your pastor asks you to help lead vacation Bible school. What do you do? If you hesitate, you're a goner. So,

> think how much better it is to say immediately, "Oh, I'd love to, but I have seven small children under four . . ."
>
> Or: "My pet ocelot died and we're holding a memorial service . . ."
>
> Or: "My invalid aunt lives with me, and she's afraid of the dark . . ."
>
> [To which the pastor says,] "Oh, that's a shame."
>
> [And you reply,] "Maybe next time. *Do* try me."

But after this happens once or twice, whenever your name is mentioned, someone will automatically

151

mumble, "Can't . . . dead ocelot . . . afraid of the dark," and pass to the next name.[1]

Now you may think these games and others like them are unique to this century, but they're not! Games were afoot among first-century believers as well. In fact, in our passage today, James introduces us to the most widely played game among Christians then and now: playing God.

It's not too difficult to figure out why we're so eager to play this game. Since the day Satan subtly manipulated Adam and Eve into playing his rebellion game, all of us have been born with a natural passion for wanting to be God in our own lives and the lives of others.

This same aggressive desire to assert ourselves is also what causes Christians to fight, as James noted earlier. He explained that, when it comes to having our desires met, we basically have two choices: we can either fight to satisfy them ourselves, or we can humbly allow God to fulfill them by surrendering to His control. James urged humility, but he knew that there were many who would choose to play God instead.

Listen carefully as James reveals the objectives and rules of this perilous game and provides a crucial evaluation of it.

When "Playing God" with Others

To begin, James addresses those whose favorite pastime is playing God with others.

The Objective

> Do not speak against one another, brethren. He who speaks against a brother, or judges his brother, speaks against the law, and judges the law; but if you judge the law, you are not a doer of the law, but a judge of it. (James 4:11)

Written between the lines of this verse is the objective of the game: imagine yourself as superior to other Christians, and put them down in various ways.

The Rules

Also found in verse 11 are the rules for playing God with others. Rule one: If you want to play God with others, you need to speak

---

1. Judi Culbertson and Patti Bard, *Games Christians Play* (New York, N.Y.: Harper and Row, Publishers, Harrow Books, 1967), pp. 8–9.

against your brother or sister. The Greek term translated "speak against" comes from a combination of two words meaning "to talk down." It's the idea of talking about one person to another with the goal of lowering your listener's estimate of that third person.

Of course, those that play this game do so only when the persons being talked about are not around to defend themselves. And there is usually little concern about accuracy. All this is neatly covered up, however, with phony words such as, "Stop me if I'm wrong, but . . ." or "Perhaps I shouldn't say this, but . . ." or "I don't mean to be critical, but . . ."

The second rule is that you must judge others. The word *judge* in verse 11 means "to pronounce condemnation upon someone." In order to judge someone rightly, however, we must know *all* there is to know about that other person. It requires the kind of complete understanding about a person's thoughts and motives that only God possesses.

Jesus condemns a judgmental attitude in his sermon on the splinter and the plank.

> "Do not judge lest you be judged. For in the way you judge, you will be judged; and by your standard of measure, it will be measured to you. And why do you look at the speck that is in your brother's eye, but do not notice the log that is in your own eye? Or how can you say to your brother, 'Let me take the speck out of your eye,' and behold, the log is in your own eye? You hypocrite, first take the log out of your own eye, and then you will see clearly to take the speck out of your brother's eye." (Matt. 7:1–5)[2]

Another reason for not judging is that when we criticize others, we speak against the law and judge it. The law James is probably referring to in chapter 4, verse 11, is the royal law he quoted in his second chapter, "You shall love your neighbor as yourself" (v. 2:8). Commentator Curtis Vaughan explains,

> The meaning is this: The man who deliberately breaks a law thereby disparages that law. In effect he sets

---

2. Jesus and James are not saying that discernment isn't necessary. They are only condemning the kind of critical attitude that *seeks* to condemn. For further study, read 1 Kings 3:9–12; Galatians 6:1; Hebrews 5:14; and James 5:19–20.

himself above it and declares that it is a bad law, not worthy to be obeyed. Such a person removes himself from the category of *a doer of the law* and becomes a *judge* of the law.[3]

The Evaluation

James now evaluates the game and states the reasons why it has no place in the believer's life.

> There is only one Lawgiver and Judge, the One who is able to save and to destroy. (4:12a)

The first reason believers should avoid playing this game is that it places us in a position of authority reserved for God alone. Only God has the ability to save and destroy, which proves that only He is qualified to judge. Second, playing God ignores or excuses our own failures.

> But who are you who judge your neighbor? (v. 12b)

In the Greek, the personal pronoun *you* is placed first in the sentence—"You there! Who are you . . . ?"—turning the spotlight away from others and putting its full force on ourselves. Commentator Donald W. Burdick writes:

> With shattering bluntness, James crushes any right his readers may have claimed to sit in judgment over their neighbors. This is not to rule out civil courts and judges. Instead, it is to root out the harsh, unkind, critical spirit that continually finds fault with others.[4]

When "Playing God" with Yourself

Perhaps the most self-deluding of all games is that version of playing God that we play out in our own lives.

The Objective

The objective for this version of playing God is written between the lines of verses 13–17. It says: Imagine yourself as the final

---

3. Curtis Vaughan, *James: A Study Guide* (Grand Rapids, Mich.: Zondervan Publishing House, 1969), pp. 93–94.

4. Donald W. Burdick, "James," in *The Expositor's Bible Commentary* (Grand Rapids, Mich.: Zondervan Publishing House, Regency Reference Library, 1981), vol. 12, p. 196.

authority over your life, then live like it. Take God completely out of the picture; don't depend on Him; don't even recognize His existence.

The Rules

Now let's examine the rules, which are revealed in verse 13.

> Come now, you who say, "Today or tomorrow, we shall go to such and such a city, and spend a year there and engage in business and make a profit."

Let's break this passage down and study the five rules we can infer from what James describes. Rule one: Selfishly choose your own time and schedule ("Come now, you who say, 'Today or tomorrow'"). Rule two: Select the location that pleases you ("we shall go to such and such a city"). Rule three: Limit your stay to please yourself ("and spend a year there"). Rule four: Arrange your activities so that they work primarily for your own benefit and pleasure ("and engage in business"). Rule five: Predict your profit and boast about it ("and make a profit").

James is not criticizing planning or advocating haphazard organization. We know from other Scriptures, such as Proverbs 18:9 and Ephesians 5:15–16, that God condones wise planning. But our plans are always to be made according to His will, acknowledging His sovereignty over our lives.

Then what is James attacking? The kind of horizontal thinking that presumptuously plans as though God did not even exist.

The Evaluation

Beginning in verse 14, James lays down several reasons why we can never win at playing God in our own lives.

> Yet you do not know what your life will be like tomorrow. (4:14a)

Tomorrow's circumstances are totally uncertain. An unexpected injury, the sudden death of a spouse, the loss of a job—these or a host of other surprises can instantly and completely change our lives. Another reason is that we have no assurance of a long life.

> What, after all, is your life? It is like a puff of smoke visible for a little while and then dissolving into thin air. (v. 14b, PHILLIPS)

Moses expressed this same truth in Psalm 90:

> You speak, and man turns back to dust. A thousand years are but as yesterday to you! They are like a single hour! We glide along the tides of time as swiftly as a racing river, and vanish as quickly as a dream. We are like grass that is green in the morning but mowed down and withered before the evening shadows fall. (vv. 3–6; LB)[5]

The third reason is that we have no right to ignore God's will.

> Instead, you ought to say, "If the Lord wills, we shall live and also do this or that." (James 4:15)

It is the height of arrogance to disregard God as the master of our fate. As Psalm 14:1 says, "The *fool* has said in his heart, 'There is no God'" (emphasis added). It's a fool's game to play God; nevertheless, James knows that some would rather take the risk and play than humbly submit to the Lord.

> But as it is, you boast in your arrogance; all such boasting is evil. (James 4:16)

Evil. All the reasons against playing this game are summed up in this one word.

When You Want to Stop "Playing God"

Quitting this game won't be easy; but for those who want out, James leaves two simple rules to follow.

> Therefore, to one who knows the right thing to do, and does not do it, to him it is sin. (v. 17)

First: *You must know the right thing to do.* You must stop and evaluate your life, whatever the cost, in light of the truth of God's Word.

Second: *You must start* doing *the right thing.* Take what you learn from studying God's Word and begin practicing it. Stop running others down and let God do the judging. Instead of seeking to control, learn to submit to God and follow.

Are you willing to stop playing God and humbly submit, instead? What are you saying in your heart right this moment? "Yes" or "Well, you know I'd really love to, but my pet ocelot just died and . . ."

---

5. See also Jesus' parable of the rich fool in Luke 12:16–21.

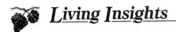

Remember walking down a game aisle in your favorite toy store when you were a child? Didn't the names Milton Bradley and Parker Brothers give you visions of wonderful hours you could spend playing games with family and friends?

Some games, however, are not mere child's play. As we have seen in our lesson, James opposes the game of playing God. And he is not alone. Another apostle, Peter, also detests this sport. Let's turn to Peter's first letter to find out how we should view and behave toward fellow Christians.

When we think of other believers, 1 Peter 1:22 says, "Since you have in obedience to the truth purified your souls for a _____

_____ of the brethren, _____ _____ one another _____

____ _____." To do this, chapter 2, verse 1 says you must first

put away all _____, _____, _____, _____, and

_____. Why is our putting away these devious gambits so

important? Perhaps because they reveal our failure to value fellow

believers as God values them, as verse 9a tells us: "But you are a

_____ _____, a _____ _____, a _____

_____, a people for God's own _____."

Since God has given you such high status, doesn't it seem incon-

sistent to devalue those whom God has honored? Peter explains to

believers, in verse 9b, why God redeemed them, "That you may

_____ the _____ of Him who has called you

out of _____ into His marvelous _____."

Hopefully, this study will convince you that you play a perilous game when you tear down another believer before others. What can you do when you're with a group who wants to play this bloody sport?

_____

_____

_____

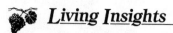

Another way to play God is to imagine yourself as your own final authority—who doesn't need to give any recognition to God. The underlying assumption is that *you* become the controller of your destiny.

Again, James 4:14 counters this perilous game: "Yet you do not know what your life will be like _____. You are just a _____ that appears for a little while and then _____ _____." Shouldn't these words cause you to look to your Creator rather than to your own resources?

The best application of this lesson, given in verse 15, is to submit all your plans to the sovereignty of Almighty God: "Instead, you ought to say, 'If the _____ wills, we shall live and also do this or that'." You may plan and carry out your daily responsibilities, but your attitude should reflect submission to God. The only alternative (v. 16) is to "_____ in your _____."

Are you playing a game where the stakes are higher than you anticipated? Playing God is perilous. It hurts those you verbally demean and removes you from God's will. Take a few moments to name the first move you are going to make to remedy this dilemma.

_____

_____

Chapter 20

WARNINGS TO THE WEALTHY
James 5:1–6

In 1923 the world's most successful financiers met at the Edgewater Beach Hotel in Chicago. Those present included the president of the largest independent steel company, the greatest wheat speculator, the president of the New York Stock Exchange, a member of the President's Cabinet, the greatest bear in Wall Street, the president of the Bank of International Settlement, and the head of the world's greatest monopoly. According to one source,

> Collectively, these tycoons controlled more wealth than there was in the United States Treasury, and for years newspapers and magazines had been printing their success stories and urging the youth of the nation to follow their examples.[1]

Two decades later a follow-up study was conducted to discover the rest of the story about these seven men who met in Chicago. The results were stunning.

> . . . the president of the largest independent steel company—lived on borrowed money for the last five years of his life, and died penniless. . . . the greatest wheat speculator—died abroad insolvent. . . . the president of the New York Stock Exchange—was released from Sing Sing. . . . the member of the President's Cabinet—was pardoned from prison so he could die at home. . . . the greatest bear in Wall Street—committed suicide. . . . the president of the Bank of International Settlement—committed suicide. . . . the head of the world's greatest monopoly—committed suicide.[2]

All seven success stories ended tragically. Names that were once synonymous with wealth, power, and influence were, in the end, associated with humiliation, crime, and violent death. It may take

---

1. Paul Lee Tan, *Encyclopedia of 7,700 Illustrations* (Rockville, Md.: Assurance Publishers, 1979), p. 824.

2. Tan, *Encyclopedia of 7,700 Illustrations*, p. 824.

intelligence to make a lot of money, but it takes even greater wisdom to handle it.

In our lesson today, it's probable that James had in mind the same kind of wealthy and influential individuals as those men who met at the Edgewater Beach Hotel. He begins chapter 5 with the sharp address, "Come now, you rich . . ."—which J. B. Phillips translates, "And now, you plutocrats . . ."

In James' day, Rome was a plutocracy—a government of the wealthy. They controlled lawyers like pawns and often caused Christians to be persecuted. Like the individuals in James 4:13 who *planned* as if there were no God, this oppressive class *spent* as though there were no God.

Introductory Clarifications

Before we begin our lesson, we need to emphasize that it is *not* true that the poor go to heaven and the rich go to hell. As simple-minded as this idea sounds, it is nevertheless a feeling common to many. However, eternal life and possessions are not that easily sorted out. In fact, there are at least four general classifications of people and possessions that we can identify.

First, *those who are poor without and within.* Poor without means they possess little of this world's goods. The millions who struggle for survival every day would be in this group. Poor within means that they are unbelievers, people who have not accepted God's priceless gift of His Son as their Savior.

Second, *those who are rich without and rich within.* These are individuals, like Joseph or Job, who were rich economically and spiritually.

Third, *those who are poor without and rich within.* These individuals have little in the way of possessions, but *are* born again. Most of us would consider ourselves in this category. We must be careful, however, that we aren't measuring what poor means by the standard of our neighbor's possessions. Are we saying we're poor because we barely have the necessities of food and shelter, or are we saying that we're poor because we have only two cars and the person next door has three and a boat?

Fourth, *those who are rich without and poor within.* This is the group James addresses—the *unbelieving* plutocrats.

Expository Instruction

Following a general rebuke in verse 1, James gives several specific statements that can be divided into two lines of thought. First, the reasons for the rebuke and, second, promises of divine judgment. Let's start with the rebuke.

General Rebuke

> Come now, you rich, weep and howl for your miseries which are coming upon you. (5:1)

With his usual frankness, James unflinchingly confronts wealthy unbelievers with their doom. He says "weep and howl," which in Greek suggests more than just a little boo-hooing; it means shrieking and loud lamentations.

Why should the rich, who have limitless power and every comfort at the tips of their bejeweled fingers, shriek and writhe in misery? James graphically reveals the reasons in his next few verses.

Human Reasons

James' first reason was that the rich were guilty of hoarding their wealth.

> Your riches have rotted and your garments have become moth-eaten. Your gold and your silver have rusted. (vv. 2–3a)

In those days, a person could display wealth basically three ways: food, clothing, and precious metals—the coin of the land. Those who were wealthy ate well, dressed extravagantly, and spent lavishly. James also introduces the three basic ways time and disuse rob a person's hoarded wealth: food rots, clothes become moth-eaten, and gold and silver tarnish. And just as riches spoil, so does the spirit of those who hoard. Time and disuse turn people's attitudes toward life into bitterness and disappointment.

The second reason the rich faced doom was because they cheated others.

> Behold, the pay of the laborers who mowed your fields, and which has been withheld by you, cries out against you; and the outcry of those who did the harvesting has reached the ears of the Lord of Sabaoth. (v. 4)

William Barclay conveys the seriousness of this crime in his illumination of this passage.

> The day labourer in Palestine lived on the very verge of starvation. His wage was small; it was impossible

for him to save anything; and if the wage was withheld from him, even for a day, he and his family simply could not eat. That is why the merciful laws of Scripture again and again insist on the prompt payment of his wages to the hired labourer. "You shall not oppress a hired servant who is poor and needy. . . . You shall give him his hire on the day he earns it, before the sun goes down (for he is poor, and sets his heart upon it); lest he cry against you to the Lord, and it be sin in you" (*Deuteronomy* 24:14, 15). . . . "Woe to him that builds his house by unrighteousness and his upper rooms by injustice; who makes his neighbour serve him for nothing, and does not give him his wages" (*Jeremiah* 22:13). "Those that oppress the hireling in his wages" are under the judgment of God (*Malachi* 3:5). . . .

. . . Here it is said that the cries of the harvesters have reached the ears of the Lord of hosts! . . . It is the teaching of the Bible in its every part that the Lord of the universe is concerned for the rights of the labouring man.[3]

Third, James rebuked the rich for living a totally selfish lifestyle.

You have lived luxuriously on the earth and led a life of wanton pleasure; you have fattened your hearts in a day of slaughter. (v. 5)

The picture James depicted here was a vivid one of unrestrained self-gratification. "Eat, drink, be merry. Get fat," and James adds, "get slaughtered."

In his commentary on James, Spiros Zodhiates writes,

When the author was in Rome, one of the most interesting places he visited was the Palace of Nero. . . . Apparently Nero and his friends liked to eat and fare sumptuously. In the middle of the main dining room was something that looked like a well. When asked what it was used for, the guide replied

3. William Barclay, *The Letters of James and Peter*, rev. ed., The Daily Study Bible series (Philadelphia, Pa.: Westminster Press, 1976), pp. 118–19.

that Nero and his guests used to eat so much that they could not hold it any more, so they had to vomit the food they just ate, and this was the place where they did it. Then back they went to the tables. . . . Such was the life of the notorious Nero. He was a man, but he lived like a pig.[4]

Those who raise livestock say that to get a pig ready for slaughter, you simply pen it up and keep shoveling in the food. Every day the pig adds more and more weight, eating itself right into the slaughterhouse. "Why should I shriek?" Nero might have sneered. Because you have satiated your stomach and your heart with this world's pleasures and starved the poor man whose work has provided your wealth, all the while ignoring the judgment that awaits this wanton self-indulgence.

The last reason for James' rebuke is that the rich were taking advantage of the righteous.

You have condemned and put to death the righteous
man; he does not resist you. (v. 6)

James has already accused the rich of dragging believers into court (2:6). Now he charges them with murder. Some teach that the righteous man refers to the Lord Jesus or the first martyr, Stephen. But the wording seems broad enough to include all the righteous who had been victimized by wealthy unbelievers.

Divine Retribution

Woven into the fabric of our passage are four promises of judgment. Let's go back to verse 1 and pick up the threads of divine retribution.

First: *Hoarded riches reap miserable dividends* (vv. 1–3a). The dividends are bitterness, cynicism, disappointment, and emptiness, to name a few. Study the selfishly wealthy and you'll see the miserable face of Charles Dickens' Ebeneezer Scrooge.

Second: *Riches provide no relief in eternity* (vv. 3b and 5b). Solomon, one of the richest men who ever lived, wrote:

Riches do not profit in the day of wrath,
But righteousness delivers from death. (Prov. 11:4)

---

4. Spiros Zodhiates, *The Behavior of Belief* (Grand Rapids, Mich.: William B. Eerdmans Publishing Co., 1959), p. 67.

After we die, God will never ask to look at the balance in our bank account. The only balance that will matter then is whether the righteousness of Christ has been credited to our account through faith in Him. Those whose accounts show only a negative balance of sin will have to pay the penalty of eternity in hell (John 3:36).

Third: *The unjust acts of the unsaved are not forgotten* (James 5:4b). One of the most serious scenes in all Scripture depicts the unsaved appearing before the Great White Throne to be judged (Rev. 20:11–15). Even though, for a little while, it may appear as if the unbelieving wealthy do not have to answer to anyone for their selfish ways, the day is coming when they will shriek in anguish as they are judged according to their deeds, which are written in God's Book.

Fourth: James implies throughout his message that *a lack of judgment today does not mean a lack of judgment tomorrow.* Jesus pictured this promise of divine judgment in the parable of the rich man and Lazarus. The rich man was poor within; he lived in luxury while Lazarus, covered with sores, begged for crumbs from his table. When death came for both, an angel took Lazarus to the bosom of Abraham, meaning heaven. While the rich man, in Hades, "lifted up his eyes, being in torment" (Luke 16:23a). Judgment had come, and it was final. Why? Because he was rich? No. Because he was an *unbeliever* while on earth. He glutted himself with perishable items while ignoring his impoverished, imperishable soul.

Applicatory Lessons

To reinforce our understanding of James' teaching, let's turn to another biblical writer, Paul, for a couple of practical lessons.

Lesson one: *God's concern is not with actual wealth, but with our attitude toward wealth.*

> And if we have food and covering, with these we shall be content. But those who want to get rich fall into temptation and a snare and many foolish and harmful desires which plunge men into ruin and destruction. For the love of money is a root of all sorts of evil, and some by longing for it have wandered away from the faith, and pierced themselves with many a pang. (1 Tim. 6:8–10)

Did you notice the two contrasting attitudes? God desires for us to possess an attitude of contentment (v. 8), not a constant craving for riches. The Lord is not condemning the rich, but He is judging those who *long* to be rich.

Lesson two: *God's counsel is not against people who are wealthy, but against the wrong priorities of the wealthy.*

> Instruct those who are rich in this present world not to be conceited or to fix their hope on the uncertainty of riches, but on God, who richly supplies us with all things to enjoy. Instruct them to do good, to be rich in good works, to be generous and ready to share, storing up for themselves the treasure of a good foundation for the future, so that they may take hold of that which is life indeed. (vv. 17–19)

Being wealthy has its own peculiar risks and pressures that twist priorities. Two that Paul mentions are becoming conceited and trusting in wealth for a sense of security. The proper priorities are fixing our hope on the Lord and being rich in good works.

Concluding Thought

Has there ever been a time in your life when you became rich within? Ephesians 1:7 says,

> In [Christ] we have redemption through His blood, the forgiveness of our trespasses, according to the riches of His grace.

For just a moment, forget about your bank account and consider your soul's account. Do you possess the riches of His grace through faith in Christ?

 Living Insights   STUDY ONE

Each of us fits into one of four categories of wealth listed at the beginning of our study. Some have few material goods and are bankrupt within. Others have both material and inward riches. There are some who are not affluent but are inwardly wealthy. And finally, many have abundant wealth but their souls are impoverished.

As we saw in our lesson, it was this last category that captured James' interest. He used four characteristics to describe these people: hoarding, cheating, living selfishly, and taking advantage of the godly. It's important to note that wealth itself is not denounced in Scripture. It is the *love* of money that is labeled evil (1 Tim. 6:10).

What is your attitude toward money? In his book *Master Your Money*, Ron Blue, a financial consultant and member of Insight for Living's Board of Directors, offers the four following guidelines to help you assess your relation to material wealth.[5] We'll explore the first two in Study One and finish up with the third and fourth in Study Two.

- *God owns it all.*

    "For it [the kingdom of heaven] is just like a man

    about to go on a journey who called his own slaves,

    and entrusted _____ possessions to _____"

    (Matt. 25:14).

As owner, God has all rights. As manager, you have responsibilities and rewards. Name a few responsibilities and rewards you have as a manager of God's resources.

_____

_____

_____

_____

- *We are in a growth process.*

    "His master said to him, 'Well done, good and

    faithful slave; you were _____ with __

    ____ _____, I will put you ____ _____

    of _____ _____'" (Matt. 25:21a).

Money is a tool to help you assume greater responsibilities. How are you becoming a better manager of your resources?

_____

_____

---

5. Ron Blue, *Master Your Money* (Nashville, Tenn.: Thomas Nelson Publishers, 1986), pp. 19–23.

What are some areas you could grow in?

_____

_____

Take some time now to map out a growth strategy.

_____

_____

_____

_____

_____

🍇 *Living Insights* _____ STUDY TWO

Let's continue our exploration from our previous study by examining Ron Blue's last two principles about how to relate to material wealth.

- *The amount is not important.*

    "He who is faithful in a _____ _____

    _____ is faithful also in _____"

    (Luke 16:10a).

In what little things have you been faithful in the past that have resulted in much?

_____

_____

What current little thing, or "very little thing," is your faithfulness being tested in?

_____

How are you doing in this area of stewardship?

_____

_____

- *Faith requires action.* In Matthew 25:24–30, the wicked slave knew what to do but didn't do it. How is your faith relating to your resources?

  _____

  _____

  _____

  _____

Chapter 21

DOING RIGHT WHEN YOU'VE BEEN DONE WRONG

James 5:7–12

Walk away," says that small but definite voice inside you.

"Wait a minute!" says a bigger voice. "That guy in the parking space next to mine just banged my car with his door!"

"Just walk away," says the persistent small voice.

"Sure, I nicked his car with my door, but it didn't even leave a mark. This guy just put one of those quarter-size dents in mine!"

"Just walk away," says the small voice, which, in spite of its size, is nonetheless getting annoying.

"I think I'll go put a couple of quarter-size dents in this guy's head!" says the big voice, sounding very mean.

"C'mon now, just walk away."

Our Natural Reaction

Walking away sounds cowardly, doesn't it? Our nature prompts us to fight back. "Revenge is a kind of wild justice,"[1] said Bacon. And Byron claimed, "Sweet is revenge."[2] Fighting back helps us get where we want to go; it helps us protect our interests and defend our territory.

But God hates retaliation games. And He sees them take place even between husband and wife, parents and children, brothers and sisters. He hates the sneaky uppercuts between boss and employee. And He especially despises the clipping He tearfully observes in the church. Oh, how He wishes we would learn how to respond when we have been done wrong.

---

1. Francis Bacon, as quoted in *The Harper Religious and Inspirational Quotation Companion*, comp. and ed. Margaret Pepper (Great Britain: André Deutsch, 1989; New York, N.Y.: Harper and Row, Publishers), p. 361.

2. Lord Byron, as quoted in *Bartlett's Familiar Quotations*, 15th ed., rev. and enl., ed. Emily Morison Beck (Boston, Mass.: Little, Brown and Co., 1980), p. 460.

God's Supernatural Alternative

God wants us to overcome our natural reaction with a *super*-natural response. We'll find out what this response is in Peter's first letter, then we'll see how to apply it in the fifth chapter of James' letter. Let's look first at Peter's counsel.

> Servants, be submissive to your masters with all respect, not only to those who are good and gentle, but also to those who are unreasonable. For this finds favor, if for the sake of conscience toward God a man bears up under sorrows when suffering unjustly. For what credit is there if, when you sin and are harshly treated, you endure it with patience? But if when you do what is right and suffer for it you patiently endure it, this finds favor with God. (1 Pet. 2:18–20)

Enduring "good and gentle" treatment is a piece of cake. And enduring suffering that comes as a result of sin is nothing extraordinary. However, enduring *unfair* treatment with patience is a novelty.

When we respond in such a supernatural way, God is pleased—Peter says twice in this passage that "this finds favor" with God (vv. 19, 20). The word for *favor* in the original Greek text is *charis*—"grace." God considers patient endurance of injustice a grace, something that is commendable because it is beyond ordinary human response.[3]

Now that we know what God expects, let's turn to James 5 to discover God's four-point plan for making this supernatural response a part of our daily experience.

Exposition of the Passage

James is placing a large package before us. When we start to open it, we'll find another package within the larger one. As we keep opening, another package and yet another will be revealed, much like a toddler's stacking cups—one inside the next. As God develops one quality in our lives toward the goal of doing right when we've been wronged, we will find that there is yet another

---

3. See Edwin A. Blum, "1 Peter," in *The Expositor's Bible Commentary* (Grand Rapids, Mich.: Zondervan Publishing House, Regency Reference Library, 1981), vol. 12, pp. 234–235.

quality to unwrap. Keep unwrapping until you have opened all four. Don't give up after opening only the first one!

General Observations

Before we tear into these packages, let's make some observations about James 5:7–12 that will give us some perspective.

First: *The passage is addressed to the believer.* The word *brethren* is mentioned four times in this passage (vv. 7, 9, 10, 12). The kind of patient endurance to which James is referring is found only in a person whose lifeline is connected to God. This is not something unbelievers can muster up themselves. God must be "mustering" it in us.

Second: *These six verses are directly related to the previous six.* As we saw in our last lesson, rich tyrants were oppressing the righteous, their treacherous acts extending all the way to murder (v. 6). Just as he finishes exposing their crimes, James turns a corner (v. 7) and begins giving the Christian victims advice on how to live in this intolerable situation.

Third: *James' advice is found in four commands—two positive and two negative.* The first two are given in a tense that essentially says, "Do this right now." The last two, being negative, are saying, "Don't even start that habit" or "Stop doing this!"

Fourth: *Woven into these verses are four vivid illustrations that shed light on each command.* Perhaps more than any other writer of Scripture, James is the most vivid illustrator. He opens the shades on the windows of our understanding to let the light pierce through, giving us no reason to miss his meaning.

Now let's look at the specifics of what he says.

Specific Explanation

Be patient. Upon opening the first package, we find that God wants us to cultivate patience.

> Be patient, therefore, brethren, until the coming
> of the Lord. (v. 7a)

In Greek, *patient* is actually a combination of two words: *makros,* meaning "a long way, far," and *thumos,* meaning "passion, heat, rage, or anger." Hence, we have the concept of "long-suffering" or taking a long time to get angry. To put it in simplest terms, patient people are not short-tempered but have a long fuse.

Two things are particularly impressive about this quality. First, it is love's first response. Remember the very first definition of love from 1 Corinthians 13? "Love is patient" (v. 4)—it "suffereth long," as the King James Version puts it. Love will motivate a person to overlook the offense, to delay the anger, to suffer long. Second, patience is essential to learning. There's an ancient Greek motto that goes something like this: "The first necessity of learning is patience." When we're irritable and impatient, we can never learn the lessons God has for us.

Now let's see how James illustrates this quality.

> Behold, the farmer waits for the precious produce of
> the soil, being patient about it, until it gets the early
> and late rains. You too be patient. (vv. 7b–8a)

Some of the richest farmland in the world is found in parts of Palestine, but most of the time—as a result of external oppression—the Jews were consigned to farming in the hill country where there was no irrigation and the soil was difficult to till. It was back-breaking work for Mr. Jewish Farmer, whose rock-tossing chores seemed never to end.

When the soil was finally prepared and the seed sown, his eyes gazed heavenward for signs of rain. After all the hard work, would the whole endeavor be for naught because of no rain? The early rains of October and November would break the stifling heat of summer and help the seed to germinate. The winter months would then bring a period of dormancy. And the latter rains, which would come in the springtime months of April and May, would allow the plants to mature. So, in order for the farmer to receive a good crop, he would have to wait. A premature planting or untimely harvest could spell disaster.

You just can't hurry God's plan.

That's why James mentions the Lord's coming back in verse 7a. He is speaking not only of the Second Coming, but also of the Lord's coming to our rescue in times when we've been wronged. And we are to be patient, just as the farmer patiently waits for God to bring rain.

Strengthen your heart. Now that we've opened James' first package, let's untie the ribbon on the second.

> Strengthen your hearts, for the coming of the Lord
> is at hand. (v. 8b)

Isn't James insightful? He knows that people who refuse to fight often retreat into their own self-pity instead of into the arms of God.

Therefore, this package is labeled "strengthen your heart."[4] The idea is "to prop up or support something that's heavy." When you've been done wrong, your heart is heavy. So James says to let the Lord support your heart and help you in this situation (see Ps. 55:22; 1 Pet. 5:7).

One way to utilize this package is through the "50:20 principle." Taken from Genesis 50:20, this principle will help you strengthen your heart by changing your focus. Let's take a brief look at the story of Joseph to uncover the specifics of this principle.

If you remember his story, you will recall the roller-coaster life Joseph had. His father's favorite son, he was also his brothers' favorite punching bag. After they sold him as a slave, he worked hard at earning his master's respect. However, he was falsely accused by the boss's wife and unjustly thrown in prison. While there, he saved a man's life, but the man quickly forgot him. Finally remembered, he interpreted Pharaoh's troubling dream and was promoted to second-in-command over all Egypt. When he eventually met his brothers again, he pronounced the words that founded the 50:20 principle:

> "And as for you, you meant evil against me, but God meant it for good . . ."

Rather than looking at ourselves or the unfair circumstances, the 50:20 principle enables us to focus on God. When we apply this guideline, we are freed up to see God as our teacher and the other person as a tool for making us into the people He intended us to be.[5]

Do not complain. So far we've opened two packages, one labeled "Be Patient" and the other labeled "Strengthen Your Hearts." Now let's take the paper off the third.

> Do not complain, brethren, against one another, that you yourselves may not be judged; behold, the Judge is standing right at the door. (James 5:9)

The word translated *complain* literally means to "groan or sigh." This groaning reveals an internal, unexpressed attitude of bearing

---

4. The phrase "strengthen your hearts," as rendered in the NASB, is the literal translation. However, the NIV helps us understand the sense of the phrase better by saying that we are to "stand firm" in the faith and not doubt that God will vindicate the righteous.

5. For another example of this principle in action, see David's response to Shimei in 2 Samuel 16.

a grudge, which is the forerunner to deep-seated bitterness and hatred. It also merits the judgment of God, who "is standing right at the door." To help us resist this grudging spirit, James uses two illustrations—first directing our attention to the Old Testament prophets and then to Job.

> As an example, brethren, of suffering and patience, take the prophets who spoke in the name of the Lord. Behold, we count those blessed who endured. (James 5:10–11a)

We need to read only a few verses of Hebrews 11 to get an idea of what the prophets had to face and how they endured. While some of them "conquered kingdoms, performed acts of righteousness," and "obtained promises" (v. 33), others "were tortured . . . experienced mockings and scourgings, yes, also chains and imprisonment. They were stoned, they were sawn in two, they were tempted, they were put to death with the sword" (vv. 35b–37a). But like Stephen, in Acts 7, these suffering saints did not dishonor God by casting blame or bearing grudges; they exemplified endurance in the midst of terrible trials. As did Job.

> You have heard of the endurance of Job and have seen the outcome of the Lord's dealings, that the Lord is full of compassion and is merciful. (James 5:11b)

William Barclay deepens our understanding of Job's endurance.

> We generally speak of the *patience* of Job which is the word the Authorized [King James] Version uses. But patience is far too passive a word. . . . As we read the tremendous drama of his life we see him passionately resenting what has come upon him, passionately questioning the conventional arguments of his so-called friends, passionately agonizing over the terrible thought that God might have forsaken him. . . . But the great fact about him is that in spite of all the agonizing questionings which tore at his heart, he never lost his faith in God. . . . "I know that my redeemer lives" (*Job* 19:25). His is no unquestioning submission; he struggled and questioned, and sometimes even defied, but the flame of his faith was never extinguished.

The word used of him is that great New Testament word . . . which describes, not a passive patience, but that gallant spirit which can breast the tides of doubt and sorrow and disaster and come out with faith still stronger on the other side. . . . It was the faith which held grimly on that came out on the other side, for "the Lord blessed the latter days of Job more than his beginning" (Job 42:12).[6]

Do not swear. And now we come to our last package of the four.

But above all, my brethren, do not swear, either by heaven or by earth or with any other oath; but let your yes be yes, and your no, no; so that you may not fall under judgment. (v. 12)

The Greek word for *swear,* as used in the New Testament, means "to grasp something sacred firmly, for the purpose of supporting what you're saying or doing." Christians shouldn't have to rely on this, because our words should be so riveted to truth that swearing or using oaths is unnecessary.

Also, in the midst of suffering it is easy to make oaths we can't keep. This is because we're caught up in the heat of the moment, eyes focused only on the present. Instead, we should wait quietly for the outcome, because that is when insight will come (see v. 11, "outcome").

And finally, James seems to be advocating plainness of speech for Christians. Rather than piously invoking a sacred presence upon all that we say, we should avoid appearing superspiritual and endure trials with humility and simplicity.

Wrapping It Up

Walking away when wronged is not a stroll in the park. It's tough, so tough that it requires supernatural empowering. That's why these four characteristics are gifts. God wishes to give you these traits so they can be a comfortable part of your attitudinal wardrobe. Try one on for size today!

6. William Barclay, *The Letters of James and Peter,* rev. ed., The Daily Study Bible series (Philadelphia, Pa.: Westminster Press, 1976), p. 125.

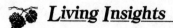

Trying out one of these four characteristics is precisely what you are asked to do today. Review the commands in this passage and write them in the spaces below.

1. Be _____. (James 5:8a)

2. _____ your _____. (v. 8b)

3. Don't _____. (v. 9)

4. Don't _____. (v. 12)

Which of these four commands do you need to put into practice most?

_____

_____

In what ways can you begin to allow God to develop the quality you mentioned above in your life? Try to give specific situations and ways in which you resolve to respond.

_____

_____

_____

_____

_____

Close in prayer, asking God to forgive you and grant you strength to respond His way.

 Living Insights   STUDY TWO

Being misunderstood is one of the hardest grievances to bear. You know you did the right thing; God knows you did the right thing. Unfortunately, no one informed everybody else! Jesus said being harshly treated by the world is par for the course.

Let's take a moment to examine two passages of Scripture in which two godly men, Jeremiah and Daniel, suffered unjustly.

Jeremiah 26:1–16, 24
Daniel 6:4–28

1. What was each man's righteous behavior?

Jeremiah _____

Daniel _____

2. What did his enemies do?

Jeremiah _____

Daniel _____

3. What was each one's response to the injustice?

Jeremiah _____

Daniel _____

4. Which of these commands do you see illustrated in each life?

Jeremiah _____

Daniel _____

Write a short prayer to the Lord asking Him to create in you the same kind of character these men of old demonstrated. Express your trust in Him to always set things right in the end.

Chapter 22

SUFFERING, SICKNESS, SIN— AND HEALING

James 5:13–16

Splash! Joni Eareckson dove into the Chesapeake Bay a strong, athletic young girl. A split second later she was paralyzed from the neck down, completely helpless, and still under water. Though rescued from drowning by her sister, the doctors could not rescue Joni from the paralysis that swept over her body.

Medically, Joni came to accept the fact that she couldn't be healed. But what about God? Didn't Christ heal all kinds of paralysis and sickness? The more Joni thought and prayed about these things, the more she became convinced God would heal her too. So,

> she brought together a group of friends and church leaders and set up a private healing service. The week before that service, she publicly confessed her faith by telling people, "Watch for me standing on your doorstep soon; I'm going to be healed." On the scheduled day the group read Scriptures, anointed her with oil and prayed in fervent faith. Today, fifteen years later, she is still a quadriplegic. . . . [She] did everything right and seemed to have met all the conditions, yet she was not healed.[1]

Was Joni denied this miracle because she didn't have enough faith? Some believe so. Others say she wasn't healed because of unconfessed sin in her life. Still others would quibble with her about the healing technique she used, saying that healing would come if she followed their three-step process.

What do *you* think?

Today thousands travel around the world seeking those who claim to have the gift of healing. Testimonies of people declaring they have been healed abound. Special "anointed" cloths are even

---

1. Bruce Barron, *The Health and Wealth Gospel* (Downers Grove, Ill.: InterVarsity Press, 1987), p. 126.

sold that are said to have healing powers. Are these things real? What about the use of medicine? Should we trust God alone for healing? What method does God honor?

What do you think? More importantly, what does God think? What process does God use to bring about healing? The answers are found in James.

Foundational Facts to Remember

Before we turn to James, however, let's take a brief look at five foundational truths undergirding our study today.

First: *There are two classifications of sin—original and personal.* Original sin refers to the sin nature we inherited from Adam (Rom. 5:12). Personal sin is the daily disobedience that is spawned by our Adamic nature (Rom. 7:14–23). Original sin is the root, personal sin is the fruit.

Second: *Original sin introduced sickness and death to the human race.* Romans 5:12 states:

Therefore, just as through one man sin entered
into the world, and death through sin, and so death
spread to all men, because all sinned.

Had Adam and Eve never sinned, they would never have died. But because they disobeyed God, sickness and death spread to every living thing. So, in the broadest sense, all sickness and death are the result of original sin.

Third: *Sometimes there is a direct relationship between personal sin and sickness.* Remember the story of David and Bathsheba in 2 Samuel 11 and 12? David committed adultery with Bathsheba, arranged for her husband to be killed, then refused to acknowledge his sin for some time. Finally, after a rebuke from the prophet Nathan, David confessed and repented. Psalm 32 is David's journal of this period. It reveals the physical sufferings he experienced while refusing to acknowledge his sin.

When I kept silent about my sin, my body wasted
away
Through my groaning all day long.
For day and night Thy hand was heavy upon me;
My vitality was drained away as with the fever
heat of summer. (vv. 3–4)

Fourth: *Sometimes there is no relationship between personal sin and sickness.* Once when the disciples and Jesus passed by a blind man, they asked,

> "Rabbi, who sinned, this man or his parents, that he should be born blind?" Jesus answered, "It was neither that this man sinned, nor his parents; but it was in order that the works of God might be displayed in him." (John 9:2b–3)

Fifth: *It is not God's will that everyone be healed.* Paul had the gift of healing (see Acts 20:7–12; 28:7–9), yet he left Trophimus sick in Miletus (2 Tim. 4:20). Epaphroditus almost died while ministering to Paul (Phil. 2:25–27). Timothy, Paul's spiritual son, had a stomach problem and "frequent ailments" (1 Tim. 5:23). Paul asked God three times to remove his "thorn in the flesh," but God said "My grace is sufficient for you" (2 Cor. 12:9b), in other words, "No."

Typically, those who claim that it is God's will for everyone to be healed base their belief upon the last phrase of Isaiah 53:5b, "And by His scourging we are healed." However, the context of this verse refers to spiritual illness and healing, not physical. Peter underscored this when he wrote,

> He Himself bore our sins in His body on the cross,
> that we might die to sin and live to righteousness;
> for by His wounds you were healed. (1 Pet. 2:24)

Scriptural Steps to Employ

With these five facts to build upon, let's listen now to James' prescription for those who are suffering, cheerful, or sick.

When We Are Suffering

> Is anyone among you suffering? Let him pray.
> (James 5:13a)

The Greek term for *suffering* here is literally "in distress." It's a broad term that can mean mental illness, anxiety, or some affliction from which there is no immediate relief. James tells this person, "Pray!" He doesn't promise that if we pray we will be healed; rather, it's as if James is exhorting us to pray for endurance—like Jesus' prayer in John 17:

> "I do not ask Thee to take them out of the world,
> but to keep them from the evil one." (v. 15)

As we learned from the lives of Paul, Trophimus, Epaphroditus, and Timothy, God sometimes chooses not to remove certain afflictions. Instead, He uses them as tools to strengthen and build us up according to His will.

When We Are Cheerful

Next, James jumps to the opposite extreme—from those who are suffering to those who are cheerful.

Is anyone cheerful? Let him sing praises. (James 5:13b)

Don't feel guilty because you're not experiencing the hardships of others. As Solomon wrote, there is "a time to weep, and a time to laugh; A time to mourn, and a time to dance" (Eccles. 3:4). If you're joyful, James says, let it out! Sing praises and thank God for the blessings He has given.

When We Are Sick

Beginning in verse 14, James introduces the problem of physical illness.

Is anyone among you sick? Let him call for the elders
of the church, and let them pray over him, anointing
him with oil in the name of the Lord.[2] (v. 14)

The Greek term for *sick* used here means "without strength." It is the idea of being totally incapacitated. What does James recommend in this situation?

First, the one who is sick should take the initiative and summon the elders of the church. There's no way anyone can know you're sick unless you tell them. And yet, many *expect* everyone to somehow know, and then they complain when nobody comes to help. When we become seriously ill, our first step is to make others aware of our needs.

Second, the elders are to carry out two functions: anoint and pray (v. 14).

---

2. Some people believe that verse 14 teaches that the clergy, namely priests, are to go to the dying and administer last rites using oil and a special liturgy. However, this passage concerns healing and not dying; restoring to health, not passing away. Others take the view that this verse applied only to the apostles of the first-century church. But James addressed elders, not apostles or "healers"; therefore, it still applies.

According to the Greek construction of the sentence, the verse actually states, "Let them pray over him, *having* anointed him with oil in the name of the Lord." The anointing should precede the praying.

Typically, the word *anoint* is associated with a religious ceremony where oil is applied to the head (see 1 Sam. 10:1). But, as Jay Adams points out in his book *Competent to Counsel,*

> James did not write about ceremonial anointing at all. . . . The ordinary word for a ceremonial anointing was *chrio* (a cognate of *christos* [Christ] the "anointed One"). The word James used (*aleipho*), in contrast to the word *chrio* ("to anoint"), usually means "to rub" or simply "apply." The word *aleipho* was used to describe the personal application of salves, lotions, and perfumes, which usually had an oil base. . . . It was even used to speak of plastering walls. . . . An *aleiptes* was a "trainer" who rubbed down athletes in a gymnastic school. *Aleipho* was used frequently in medical treatises. And so it turns out that what James required by the use of oil was the use of the best medical means of the day. James simply said to rub oil . . . on the body, and pray. . . . In this passage he urged the treating of sickness by medical means accompanied by prayer. The two are to be used together; neither to the exclusion of the other. So instead of teaching faith healing apart from the use of medicine, the passage teaches just the opposite.[3]

Fortunately, our medical expertise has improved from oil to antibiotics, X rays, and laser surgery. And just as the elders in James' day were to see that proper medical treatment was applied, the same is true of elders today.

Third, James recommends that the sick leave the results in God's hands. The elders were to anoint and pray over the sick "in the name of the Lord" (v. 14b), invoking God's will for the situation. And that prayer of faith leads to three specific results, found in verse 15.

---

3. Jay Adams, *Competent to Counsel* (Phillipsburg, N.J.: Presbyterian and Reformed Publishing Co., 1970), pp. 107–8. Compare Mark 16:1 and John 12:3, regarding ceremonial anointing, with Luke 10:33b–34a, which refers to medical anointing.

The prayer offered in faith will restore the one who is sick, and the Lord will raise him up, and if he has committed sins, they will be forgiven him.

The three specific results James mentions are restoration, raising up, and forgiveness. Yes, he addresses the sins of the sick person too. The context clearly indicates that this is a person who is suffering physically as a direct result of personal sin. Evidence for this is found in the Greek word for *restoration, sōzō,* meaning "saved." It's the same word James uses in verse 20.

Let him know that he who turns a sinner from the error of his way will save his soul from death, and will cover a multitude of sins.

Saving "his soul from death" is a reference to restoring someone's fellowship with God. When James says in verse 15 that the prayer offered in faith will *restore* the one who is sick, he means restoring that individual's spiritual life.

The next result is that the Lord will raise this individual up (James 5:15), which refers to physical healing. If a person is physically ill due to unconfessed sin, then by confessing that sin, he or she can be healed physically.[4]

The final result of confessing is God's gracious forgiveness.

Practical Principles to Claim

In summary, let's glean four practical measures to follow—two from verse 16 and two from our passage as a whole.

Therefore, confess your sins to one another, and pray for one another, so that you may be healed. The effective prayer of a righteous man can accomplish much. (v. 16)

First: *Confession of sin is healthy—employ it!* Don't let sins build up in your life to the point that they make you physically ill. William Barclay writes,

In a very real sense it is easier to confess sins to God than it is to confess them to men; and yet in sin

---

4. God does promise to raise up this individual, but He does not commit Himself to a specific time. The healing may be instantaneous or it may take weeks, months, or years—or it may not take place until we begin living in eternity with Him.

there are two barriers to be removed—the barrier it sets up between us and God, and the barrier it sets up between us and our fellow-men. If both these barriers are to be removed, both kinds of confession must be made.[5]

Second: *Praying for one another is essential—practice it!* An appropriate response to your friends' confessions would be to lift them up to the Lord in prayer. Let these companions know that you are willing to enter into their struggle; let them hear your love and support being poured out on their behalf before the throne of God.

Third: *Use of medical assistance is imperative—obey it!* Asking others to pray for your physical healing while ignoring proper medical treatment is not spiritual, it's foolish. Someone may rightly ask, "Why should I pray for your healing if you're not willing to do all that God commands, like seeking medical assistance?

Fourth: *When healing comes from God—claim it!* Whether or not an illness is the result of personal sin, when God heals, remember to thank Him and give Him the glory!

A Final Word

Did you notice that James never once mentions faith healers? When we're sick, we are commanded to call for the leaders in our local assembly. And it makes no difference what their spiritual gifts are.

In conclusion, let me summarize my own convictions on this important topic.

> I believe in divine healing. I do not believe in divine healers. I believe in faith healing. I do not believe in faith healers. There is a great difference. I believe that God in His sovereign grace and power will in fact reach down in some cases and change a condition. . . . And I am of the conviction that God does that apart from any individual who claims to have certain powers.[6]

---

5. William Barclay, *The Letters of James and Peter,* rev. ed., The Daily Study Bible series (Philadelphia, Pa.: Westminster Press, 1976), p. 131.

6. Charles R. Swindoll, "Suffering, Sickness, Sin—and Healing." Sermon given at the First Evangelical Free Church of Fullerton, California, January 5, 1975.

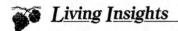 *Living Insights* STUDY ONE

Let's take another look at the issues of suffering, sickness, sin, and healing, this time personalizing James' remarks.

Are you suffering? If your circumstances are pressing you hard, then James encourages you to pray and to endure. If you were to compare yourself to an athlete, would you say you are capable of enduring a marathon of suffering, or are you out of breath after only a few strides?

_____

If you need to build up your endurance, take some time to meditate on and memorize the following passages: Romans 5:3–5, James 1:2–4, and Isaiah 40:31. For further study, read Philip Yancey's book *Where Is God When It Hurts?*

Are you cheerful? You are free to _____ (James 5:13b). You needn't feel guilty for not having the hardships others experience. What are some other ways you can express the joy God has given you?

_____

_____

_____

Are you struggling with major or prolonged sickness? Have you followed James' prescription: (1) make others aware of your situation, (2) seek medical attention, and (3) ask the elders of your church to pray over you? Take a moment or two to evaluate your own situation and see if you have overlooked any of James' recommendations.

 Living Insights STUDY TWO

If you are struggling with sickness even after following James' three-part prescription, perhaps you need to look at his fourth word of counsel—confession of sin. Could personal sin be the cause of some of your physical problems? Have repressed anger or jealousy caused you some sleepless nights, headaches, ulcers, or anxiety attacks?

To help diagnose your condition, set aside some time to pray through David's words in Psalm 139, and search your own heart and thoughts for any "hurtful way" that needs to be confessed.

> Search me, O God, and know my heart;
> Try me and know my anxious thoughts;
> And see if there be any hurtful way in me,
> And lead me in the everlasting way. (vv. 23–24)

For those of you who are in the merciless hands of an unrelenting illness, please know that we are not assuming that personal sin is the root of all suffering. As we saw clearly in our lesson, there is sometimes no relationship between sin and sickness. Rather, God may be using our physical sufferings to display His works in us.

> And as He passed by, He saw a man blind from birth. And His disciples asked Him, saying, "Rabbi, who sinned, this man or his parents, that he should be born blind?" Jesus answered, "It was neither that this man sinned, nor his parents; but it was in order that the works of God might be displayed in him." (John 9:1–3)

What is God displaying through your sickness or affliction?

_____

_____

_____

_____

If you're having trouble understanding God's work in your life, let the apostle Paul show you what he discovered regarding his circumstances . . . and maybe you'll be able to find them in yours too.

> There was given me a thorn in the flesh. . . . Concerning this I entreated the Lord three times that it might depart from me. And He has said to me, "My grace is sufficient for you, for power is perfected in weakness." (2 Cor. 12:7b–9a)

May God grant that you will see His grace and power revealed through your weakness.

Chapter 23

THE POWER
OF EFFECTIVE KNEELING

James 5:13–18

As far as nicknames go, there aren't many people who would
want to be known as "Ol' Camel Knees." But that's exactly
what James' friends respectfully called him. And the reason might
surprise you, especially since his letter emphasizes the practical
aspects of the Christian life. Herbert Lockyer, in his book *All the
Men of the Bible,* writes that James

> was a man who believed in the power of prayer. . . .
> Because of his habit of always kneeling in interces-
> sion for the saints, his knees became calloused like
> a camel's; thus he became known as "The Man with
> Camel's Knees."[1]

James was a man of action—a diligent, practical-thinking Christian. But he was also a man of prayer. He marched forth on his
knees, taking heaven by storm with fervent, bold, effective prayer.

In our last lesson, we studied the advice of the practical-thinking
James on suffering, sickness, sin, and healing. Today, let's go back
and note the exhortation of the camel-kneed James on "the power
of effective kneeling."

Instruction of James

The thread of prayer woven into the letter of James begins in
chapter 1. Looking back, you may recall the advice James gave
those whose faith was being tested and who needed help to endure.

> But if any of you lacks wisdom, let him ask of
> God, who gives to all men generously and without
> reproach, and it will be given to him. (James 1:5)

Later, in chapter 4, prayer emerges again, but this time in a
context of conflict.

---

1. Herbert Lockyer, *All the Men of the Bible* (Grand Rapids, Mich.: Zondervan Publishing
House, 1958), p. 171.

What is the source of quarrels and conflicts among you? Is not the source your pleasures that wage war in your members? You lust and do not have; so you commit murder. And you are envious and cannot obtain; so you fight and quarrel. You do not have because you do not ask. (4:1–2)

It's sad to think how many of us could confess the truth of this last part of verse 2, isn't it? Someone once pictured heaven as having an enormous room with brightly wrapped and beribboned packages in it, each gift having one of our names on it and a little tag that says, "Never delivered to earth, because never requested from earth."

Over and over again in Scripture, we are shown that God wants us to ask because He wants us to have (see Matt. 7:7–11; Heb. 4:16). The topic of our passage today is the matter of asking God certain things because of certain situations.

So let's look at this passage, James 5:13–18, six verses where prayer is mentioned seven times. Within these verses, James brings before us four practical areas where prayer is essential.

When Afflicted . . . Pray!

Is anyone among you suffering? Let him pray. (v. 13a)

As we noted in our last lesson, the Greek term for *suffering* here is a broad one that includes not only physical suffering but mental and emotional anguish as well. For those who are in this crucible of pain, James' counsel is to respond not with complaints (v. 9) or swearing (v. 12), but with continual prayer.[2]

What can we expect in return for our prayers? It's important to note that James does not promise specific relief, although relief may come. Nor does he guarantee that we will understand the reason behind our suffering. So why pray? Are our hot tears and pained cries all in vain? C. H. Spurgeon addressed this question.

We ought not to tolerate for a minute the ghastly and grievous thought that God will not answer prayer. His *nature,* as manifested in Christ Jesus, demands it. He has revealed Himself in the gospel, as a God

---

2. The command to pray is in the present tense, which signifies to pray continuously.

of love, full of grace and truth; and how can He refuse to help those of His creatures who humbly in His
own appointed way seek His face and favour? . . .

Still remember that prayer is always to be offered
in submission to God's will; that when we say, God
heareth prayer, we do not intend by that, that He always gives us literally what we ask for. We do mean,
however, this, that He gives us what is best for us;
and that if He does not give us the mercy we ask
for in silver, He bestows it upon us in gold. If He
doth not take away the thorn in the flesh, yet He
saith, "My grace is sufficient for thee," and that
comes to the same in the end.[3]

So the role of prayer in our suffering is to place the aching
burden into the tender hands of God, who will in turn renew our
inner strength and make the load easier to bear.

When Sick . . . Pray!

The second situation in which James calls for prayer involves
those who are bedridden and without strength due to a serious physical illness.

Is anyone among you sick? Let him call for the elders
of the church, and let them pray over him, anointing
him with oil in the name of the Lord. (v. 14)

If we're sick, we should follow three steps, according to this
verse. First, we should make the spiritual leaders of the church
aware of our need.

Second, and this step is rooted in the word *anoint*, we should
see a doctor and ask for prayer. In our last lesson we saw that the
Greek term for *anointing* here refers to rubbing in oil for medicinal
purposes. So in James' day this meant that the leaders were to come
and administer two things: proper medicine and prayer. And for us
today, James is simply saying that the elders should make sure we're
getting proper medical treatment and pray for us.

Third, because the medical treatment and prayer for healing
should be done "in the name of the Lord," we need to leave the
results of the medicine and prayers in God's hands.

---

3. C. H. Spurgeon, "The Golden Key of Prayer," in *Twelve Sermons on Prayer* (Grand Rapids,
Mich.: Baker Book House, 1990), pp. 10, 13.

When Corrupted by Sin . . . Pray!

> Therefore, confess your sins to one another, and pray
> for one another, so that you may be healed. (v. 16a)

Remember, James has just dealt with those who were bedridden. According to the context of verses 13–16, these people were ill as a result of unconfessed sin in their lives. Beginning in verse 16, however, James turns a corner, as evidenced by his use of "therefore" and his switch from "him" to "you." *Therefore* lets us know that James is about to make an important point, and *you* takes this point out of the theoretical and into the personal. In short, James is advising that, to keep sin from making us ill, we need to *confess* our sins to one another regularly and *pray* continuously.

Before we move to the next point in our study, let's pause for a moment to remove some theological barnacles that have accumulated on the timeless truth of verse 16.

Briefly, there are some who say that this verse is talking about salvation. However, James is addressing believers, and the subject is healing. Others teach that we should confess our sins *only* to the Lord. Yet James clearly says to confess our sins to "one another." Still others teach that verse 16 is talking about confession to a priest. But the words "one another" show that James simply means believers. Finally, James is recommending that we not bare our sins indiscriminately before an entire group. There is a tone of privacy in his "one another" counsel. There are certain matters we should not suffer alone. They should be shared and prayed about with a close brother or sister.

When Specific Needs Occur . . . Pray!

James reveals the last area in which prayer is essential in the second half of verse 16:

> The effective prayer of a righteous man can accomplish much.

The Greek term for *prayer* used here is *deēsis,* meaning "specific prayer based on specific needs." It's the only time in his letter that James uses this word.

In addition, he intensifies his statement by using two qualifying adjectives, *effective* and *much.* The Greek root for effective is *energeō,* from which we get the word *energy.* It has to do with adding an ingredient that turns something average into something fantastic.

For instance, if a speech is lacking *energeō*, it's just another speech. But if a speech has this quality, it's dynamite!

So what does it mean to pray "effectively?" It involves knowing and praying in accordance with Scripture. It also includes being specific. Learn to deal directly with the issues you pray about by asking for specific results. This does not mean, however, that we require God to meet our deadlines. Faith involves waiting on God's timing without doubting. And finally, *energeō* prayer embraces an absolute and unshakable faith that God hears and answers prayer.

The result of effective prayer is that it will "accomplish much," just as it did in Elijah's life.

> Elijah was a man with a nature like ours, and he prayed earnestly that it might not rain; and it did not rain on the earth for three years and six months. And he prayed again, and the sky poured rain, and the earth produced its fruit. (vv. 17–18)

Elijah was cut out of the same cloth as the rest of us. The only difference between Elijah and many of us is that he practiced effective praying—he prayed in accordance with God's will, he was specific, and he prayed in faith (see 1 Kings 17–18).

The Relevance of James

Looking back on these major areas of prayer that James mentioned, we can find four specific applications for us today.

First: *Prayer is to be continuous.* Prayer is not something we should practice only at mealtimes or in moments of panic or when we've exhausted all of our own efforts to meet our needs. James repeatedly used the present tense throughout these verses, exhorting us to pray continuously or, as the apostle Paul said, "without ceasing" (1 Thess. 5:17). The adverb for *ceasing* in Greek is like a hacking cough—something that you are constantly reminded of throughout the day. The Puritans described this kind of constant prayerful attitude as practicing the presence of God—keeping alert to His presence throughout the day.

Second: *Prayer is designed for every part of life.* Affliction, sickness, sin, specific needs—nothing is too big or too small for prayer. If it's a concern—ask!

Third: *Prayer is not a substitute for responsible and intelligent action.* Remember that the one who is sick is supposed to contact the elders and seek proper medical treatment. If you're not willing to see a doctor and take the right kind of medicine, don't ask people to pray for you. And remember that healing some physical illnesses may involve confessing sins and seeking forgiveness.

Fourth: *Prayer is not for the perfect, but the imperfect.* Because we are imperfect and have needs, we need to pray. Elijah wasn't perfect, but he was persistent about prayer. So was James—"Ol' Camel Knees." What nickname would you use to describe yourself in light of your prayer life?

Before we close and the daily demands of your life distract you from what you've just learned, pause and meditate on these powerful words from Clarence Edward Macartney:

> What is the word that unites far separated souls around one common mercy seat? What is the word that brings man's storm-driven ship into the haven of safety and peace? What is the word that turns back the shadow of death on the face of life's dial? What is the word that gives songs in the night and that lifts the load of guilt from the conscience-smitten heart? What is the word that puts a sword in our hand when we face temptation? What is the word that gives us strength to bear our daily burdens? . . . What is the word that makes us co-workers with God in the coming of His kingdom? . . .
>
> . . . What is the word that companions the soul in its hours of loneliness and that comforts it in the day of sorrow? What is the word that sets a lamp of forgiveness and reconciliation in the window for the prodigal and the wanderer? What is the word that brings the eternal world to view? . . . What is the word that makes the angels rejoice when they hear it on the lips of a contrite sinner? . . .
>
> That mighty, all prevailing, God-conquering word is prayer. *"The effectual fervent prayer of a righteous man availeth much"* (James 5:16).[4]

---

4. Clarence Edward Macartney, "The Word That Conquers God," in *Classic Sermons on Prayer,* comp. Warren W. Wiersbe (Grand Rapids, Mich.: Kregel Publications, 1987), pp. 9–10.

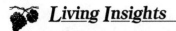

Living Insights

"You do not have because you do not ask (4:2)." How many of us spend time laboring over something or worrying about it or becoming preoccupied with it . . . only to realize later that we've hardly prayed for it?

A story is told of a good-hearted minister who wanted to teach his congregation about prayer. He spent weeks researching and studying and writing, until finally his lesson was complete. On Sunday he stepped up to the pulpit, notes and quotes in hand, and it suddenly struck him that he'd left out one vital step of preparation. He'd forgotten to pray for his sermon on prayer.

How many vital concerns have we forgotten to pray about?

Take a moment to think through some of the desires and concerns that have been on your heart. Have they also been in your prayers? In the space provided, write down a few of these unprayed-for concerns.

_____ _____

_____ _____

_____ _____

Put these concerns on a three-by-five-inch card, and keep that card with you in your car, at work, at home—wherever you may be—as a reminder to pray more often so that you *can* have because you *do* ask.

Living Insights

Sometimes we do ask earnestly, with the right motives, but we still do not have the answer that we seek. During these times, God seems silent, uncaring, deaf to our prayers. But this is not the case at all, as Hannah would testify (see 1 Sam. 1–2:11).

> If Hannah's prayer for a son had been answered at the time she set for herself, the nation might never have known the mighty man of God it found in Samuel. Hannah wanted only a son, but God wanted more. He wanted a prophet, and a saviour, and a ruler for His people. Someone said that "God had

to get a woman before He could get a man." This woman He got in Hannah precisely by delaying the answer to her prayer, for out of the discipline of those weeks and months and years there came a woman with a vision like God's, with tempered soul and gentle spirit and a seasoned will prepared to be the kind of a mother for the kind of a man God knew the nation needed.[5]

Take heart. God does hear and care about your prayers, because He *is* at work—even when we can't see or comprehend it.

5. W. E. Biederwolf, as quoted in A *Treasury of Prayer: The Best of E. M. Bounds on Prayer in a Single Volume*, compiled and condensed by Leonard Ravenhill (Minneapolis, Minn.: Bethany House Publishers, 1961), p. 176.

Chapter 24

HOW TO HANDLE
STRAYING SAINTS
James 5:19–20

Have you ever rescued someone from drowning? If so, you know how victims often fight their rescuers in the hysteria of that terrifying moment. The same is often true when an attempt is made to rescue those who are floundering spiritually because their faith has suffered shipwreck.

Author and teacher Howard Hendricks tells the story of a young man who strayed from the Lord but was finally brought back by the help of a friend who really loved him. When there was full repentance and restoration, Dr. Hendricks asked this Christian how it felt while he was away from God. The young man said that it seemed like he was out at sea, in deep water, deep trouble, and all his friends were on the shoreline hurling biblical accusations at him about justice, penalty, and wrong.

"But there was one Christian brother who actually swam out to get me and would not let me go. I fought him, but he pushed aside my fighting, grasped me, put a life jacket around me, and took me to shore. By the grace of God, he was the reason I was restored. He would not let me go."[1]

James doesn't want us to let anyone go either. Throughout his epistle, he has stressed the need for a faith that works. Now he reminds us not to let go of those who have grown weary and strayed.

Comparing James with Jesus

As a backdrop to our study today, let's compare James' and Jesus' teachings on the subject of judging. To start, turn back to James 4:11–12.

> Do not speak against one another, brethren. He
> who speaks against a brother, or judges his brother,

---

1. As retold by Charles R. Swindoll, in a sermon titled "Set Me Free," given at the First Evangelical Free Church of Fullerton, California, January 25, 1981.

speaks against the law, and judges the law; but if you judge the law, you are not a doer of the law, but a judge of it. There is only one Lawgiver and Judge, the One who is able to save and to destroy; but who are you who judge your neighbor?

In this passage, James is not prohibiting Christians from confronting those who have strayed; rather, he is warning against believers who maliciously slander others. Jesus underscored this same point in Matthew 7:

> "Do not judge lest you be judged. For in the way you judge, you will be judged; and by your standard of measure, it will be measured to you. And why do you look at the speck that is in your brother's eye, but do not notice the log that is in your own eye? Or how can you say to your brother, 'Let me take the speck out of your eye,' and behold, the log is in your own eye?" (vv. 1–4)

The conclusion many Christians have drawn from these passages can be boiled down to just three words: Do not judge!

But what about those times when a Christian brother or sister strays from the Lord? Shouldn't we attempt to rescue those whose faith has suffered shipwreck? Or do we simply let them perish? The climax of Jesus' words in our Matthew passage answers this seeming dilemma.

> "You hypocrite, first take the log out of your own eye, and then you will see clearly to take the speck out of your brother's eye." (v. 5)

According to Jesus, there *is* a place for taking specks out of other Christians' eyes. But remember, there are few places in our bodies more sensitive to touch than the eye. And just as removing something from the eye requires extreme sensitivity, so does attempting to remove the spiritual speck from our brother's or sister's eye. So Jesus is not condoning those who feel "called" to criticism. Rather, He is welcoming the help of those who are willing to have their own spiritual eyes cleared before rescuing others.

Understanding James' Counsel

To learn more about the techniques involved in spiritual eye surgery, let's turn now to James' closing words.

> My brethren, if any among you strays from the
> truth, and one turns him back, let him know that
> he who turns a sinner from the error of his way will
> save his soul from death, and will cover a multitude
> of sins. (James 5:19–20)

Four important questions arise from these verses.

Important Questions

First: To whom is the counsel addressed? At a glance, it appears as though James is speaking about saving lost souls from hell. However, the words "my brethren" and "among you" indicate that he is addressing believers.

Second: What has occurred that would cause James to write these words? Most likely, someone has strayed from the truth. The word *strays* in Greek is *planaō*, from which we get the word planet. The heavenly bodies seemed to the ancient Greeks to wander in the sky. Likewise, when Christians stray from the truth, they wander from the prescribed course they once knew.[2]

Third: From what has the person strayed? The truth. Commentator Spiros Zodhiates expands on what straying from the truth involves.

> The truth of which James speaks is naturally the
> person and work of Jesus Christ. He does not refer
> to an abstract philosophical or theological system,
> but to Christ Himself, who said, "I am the way, the
> truth, and the life" (John 14:6). . . . Of course, the
> word "truth" here also means all that Christ taught
> and instituted. It is His whole doctrinal and prac-
> tical teaching—not the teaching of any particular
> church or denomination, but of Christ. And where
> is this teaching to be found? In the Word of God,
> in the Bible.[3]

Fourth: What should be done? Now we come to the most sensitive part: removing the speck from our brother's eye. When Chris-

---

2. Again, the implication here is that James is talking to believers, because only those who have intimately known the truth can stray from it. Unbelievers cannot stray from something they have never known.

3. Spiros Zodhiates, *The Behavior of Belief* (Grand Rapids, Mich.: William B. Eerdmans Publishing Co., 1959), p. 217.

tians willfully stray from the truth, James says that one must turn them back, meaning *any* Christian with a clear eye—not just church leaders—must help turn around those who stray. Don't ignore them or hurl criticisms from a distance, as some did to that young Christian Dr. Hendricks has talked about. Swim out after them and don't let them go!

Proper Attitude

Now that we've considered the action we must take, let's turn to Galatians 6 for a close look at the proper attitude we need.

> Brethren, even if a man is caught in any trespass, you who are spiritual, restore such a one in a spirit of gentleness; each one looking to yourself, lest you too be tempted. Bear one another's burdens, and thus fulfill the law of Christ. For if anyone thinks he is something when he is nothing, he deceives himself. (Gal. 6:1–3)

To qualify for helping restore others to the truth, we must first be filled with the Spirit and not controlled by the flesh. We must seek the Spirit's help in removing the logs in our own eyes before we attempt to remove them from others'. Only those who are spiritual —who approach such an operation in complete dependence upon the Spirit—need apply for the job.

The second qualification Paul mentions is gentleness. Carnal Christians are usually extremely sensitive to criticism. To approach them with a harsh, critical spirit only ensures failure and rejection. But a gentle spirit encourages those who are floundering to relax and be reconciled to God.

Third, before we rush off into deep water to rescue someone, we should check to be sure we are equipped with an attitude of humility—"looking to yourself, lest you too be tempted." Misjudging the depth of the problem or overestimating our ability to handle it could quickly leave *us* floundering as well.

Removing specks is not a pleasurable task. There's no delight in rescuing someone who is thrashing and kicking against your every effort to help. In fact, those who are truly humble are often reluctant to step in, knowing that they don't have the power in themselves to pull the other person to safety. But, nevertheless, the humble do wade out, slowly . . . prayerfully, because of a genuine love from the Father (Gal. 6:2).

Thus far we've covered the action and attitude involved in handling saints who stray. Now let's go back to James 5 and see what happens when they are restored.

> Let him know that he who turns a sinner from the
> error of his way will save his soul from death, and
> will cover a multitude of sins. (James 5:20)

The first result is that the straying saint's soul will be saved "from death." The word *death* could mean that if this individual had not turned back to the Lord, he or she may have died under divine discipline. It is more likely, however, that James means death in a broad, metaphorical sense. When we turn straying saints back to the Lord, we rescue their souls from a deathlike existence of loneliness, bitterness, anguish, and guilt.

The second result is that we "cover a multitude of sins." When someone is brought back into the fold through confession and repentance, Christ's forgiveness covers this formerly lost sheep completely.

Summary and Application

All through his letter James has pinpointed specific areas in which Christians have begun to slip. For example: doubting during trials, passing the buck when tempted, anger and prejudice, sterile intellectualism, a loose tongue, jealousy, arrogance, being judgmental, planning without God, taking advantage of others because of wealth, and lack of prayer—to name a few. For these five chapters, James has been coming to our rescue. Now let's close by crystallizing his counsel about our rescuing one another.

First, there are definite occasions when we are to be involved in removing specks from others' eyes. Second, the entire process must be under the direction of the Holy Spirit. Third, the motive or attitude is as important as the action. And fourth, when we are prompted by the Lord, we should not feel reluctant or out of place about confronting others. Remember that you are saving that person from death and covering a multitude of sins. Don't let go!

Living Insights

STUDY ONE

In Matthew 7:1–2, Jesus clearly commands us not to condemn another person. And yet He doesn't command us to condone another person's sin either. According to verse 5, what do you need to do before you address another person's fault?

_____

_____

James and Jesus qualify the preparatory *action* necessary for confronting another person. In Galatians 6:1, however, Paul circles the mandatory *attitude* needed to bring about restoration of a person whose fellowship with God has been broken.

> Brethren, even if a man is caught in any trespass,
> you who are spiritual, restore such a one in a spirit
> of gentleness; each one looking to yourself, lest you
> too be tempted.

Are you considering confronting someone? This passage contains three conditions we need to meet in order to be qualified to confront others who are in sin.

- *Spiritual.* What does a spiritual attitude look like? Take a moment to study Galatians 5:22–23, James 3:17, and 1 Corinthians 13 to gather details for this portrait.

_____

_____

_____

_____

- *Gentle.* Let's turn to the Scriptures for some examples of gentleness. Review Matthew 21:5, 11:29, 5:5, and John 8:1–11. What does Jesus teach you about this tender trait?

_____

_____

_____

200

Has someone in your life modeled this character trait for you? How? In what way did it affect you?

_____

_____

_____

_____

_____

_____

_____

- *Humble.* Jesus said,

> "You know that the rulers of the Gentiles lord it over them, and their great men exercise authority over them. It is not so among you, but whoever wishes to become great among you shall be your servant, and whoever wishes to be first among you shall be your slave; just as the Son of Man did not come to be served, but to serve, and to give His life a ransom for many." (Matt. 20:25b–28)

What's your motive in confronting other people? Is it to put them down, to get even, to exalt yourself as holier than thou? Or is it to serve them, to seek their best?

As you search your heart, meditate and pray through these words of the apostle Paul.

> And so, as those who have been chosen of God, holy and beloved, put on a heart of compassion, kindness, humility, gentleness and patience; bearing with one another, and forgiving each other, whoever has a complaint against anyone; just as the Lord forgave you, so also should you. And beyond all these things put on love, which is the perfect bond of unity. (Col. 3:12–14)

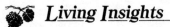

Living Insights STUDY TWO

James has brought us through some rough terrain. He first led us through trials, then temptations, through valleys of prejudice, and into flaming forests of fiery words. The perishing palaces of the wealthy were on one side of the road, while the humble houses of the righteous lay on the other. Up we went onto a peak of prayer, and then we wound up our journey in a cove of compassionate grace.

Now that our travels through James have come to an end, take some time to collect your thoughts by writing a brief journal entry on the truths you gathered along the way.

_____

_____

_____

_____

_____

_____

_____

_____

_____

_____

_____

_____

_____

BOOKS FOR PROBING FURTHER

Practice, practice, practice. When you sign on to study James, you'd better be prepared to face one of the toughest drill instructors on the Christian life that has ever lived. His boot camp epistle is dedicated to turning lackadaisical hearers of the Word into committed doers. Just give him five chapters and he'll give you some of the best basic training available for practicing your faith.

If James has challenged you to grow, to mature, you may want to extend your stay in his book. Or if you'd like to pursue some of the topics discussed in it, we would highly recommend these books.

Commentaries on James

Barclay, William. *The Letters of James and Peter.* Revised edition. The Daily Study Bible series. Philadelphia, Pa.: Westminster Press, 1976. A wellspring of insight and illumination, Barclay's work gives us a deeper understanding of the message of James and how to apply it. An excellent resource.

Burdick, Donald W. "James." In *The Expositor's Bible Commentary.* Volume 12. Grand Rapids, Mich.: Zondervan Publishing House, Regency Reference Library, 1981. This work is a solid reference tool for the layperson or pastor. Burdick examines James' epistle verse by verse and includes helpful translations of key Greek words and phrases.

Vaughan, Curtis. *James.* Grand Rapids, Mich.: Zondervan Publishing House, 1969. This small volume acts as a guide for anyone who wants to understand the message of James' epistle. Its features include an outline of the book of James, illuminating translations of pertinent Greek words and phrases, a wide array of quotes from other authors and Bible versions, and thorough explanations of James' stern words.

Zodhiates, Spiros. *The Behavior of Belief.* Grand Rapids, Mich.: William B. Eerdmans Publishing Co., 1959. With close attention to the original language and James' intended meanings, Spiros Zodhiates has written one of the most extended expository studies on the book of James. His purpose was to help touch and influence those who read James and he has done just that. The writing is clear, informative, and just as practical as the book he interprets.

Books That Focus on Key Themes in James

Colson, Charles. *Kingdoms in Conflict.* Grand Rapids, Mich.: William Morrow and Zondervan Publishing House, 1987. This stimulating and well-written book encourages us to exhibit an active faith through social action. Colson examines such timely issues as the separation of church and state, the role of Christians in politics, and civil disobedience. His style is clear, literate, and intelligent, and his book is a valuable resource for the thinking Christian.

————. *Loving God.* Grand Rapids, Mich.: Zondervan Publishing House, 1983. James writes, "Draw near to God and He will draw near to you" (James 4:8a). In this penetrating and challenging book by Chuck Colson, you will learn how to draw near to God and discover what it really means to love Him.

Geisler, Norman L. *Christian Ethics.* Grand Rapids, Mich.: Baker Book House, 1989. The author writes in his preface, "More than ever before, we need to bring the standard of God's revealed truth to bear on the . . . moral problems that confront a Christian in our contemporary culture." This straightforward and thorough book examines such issues as abortion, war, ecology, and marriage and divorce.

Hunter, W. Bingham. *The God Who Hears.* Downers Grove, Ill.: InterVarsity Press, 1986. Are faithful prayers always answered? Why pray to a God who lets people hurt? Does prayer change God's mind? How can I be intimate with an invisible God? W. Bingham Hunter tackles these and other pressing questions in his excellent study on prayer.

Mains, Karen Burton. *You Are What You Say.* Grand Rapids, Mich.: Zondervan Publishing House, 1988. Subtitled *Cure for the Troublesome Tongue,* this book can help you transform an unruly tongue into a tool for God's glory. Mains assists you in diagnosing what kind of trouble you're having, then she presents some "surgeries" and "rehabilitations" that will profoundly impact your speech and your view of the power of words.

Neff, David, ed. *The Midas Trap.* The Christianity Today Series. Wheaton, Ill.: Victor Books, 1990. James writes of the rich man, "Like flowering grass he will pass away . . . in the midst of his pursuits [he] will fade away" (James 1:10b–11). Despite James' sobering observations, many Christians in today's world are intoxicated with the promises of wealth. In Neff's book, leading Christian thinkers look intently at what the New Testament says about this topic and explain how the Spirit can free us from the pressures and seductions of material wealth.

Stott, John. *Involvement.* Volume 1, *Being a Responsible Christian in a Non-Christian Society.* A Crucial Questions Book. Old Tappan, N.J.: Fleming H. Revell Co., 1985. John Stott challenges us to meet the crises of our time with a "Christian mind" and to display Christ's love through active involvement in the world.

———. *Involvement.* Volume 2, *Social and Sexual Relationships in the Modern World.* A Crucial Questions Book. Old Tappan, N.J.: Fleming H. Revell Co., 1985. In this companion volume, Stott explores contemporary moral and social issues and sets forth the basis for effective Christian response.

Wright, H. Norman. *Communication: Key to Your Marriage.* Glendale, Calif.: G/L Publications, Regal Books, 1974. Married or single, this book is tremendously valuable for improving your ability to communicate. It is warm, personal, and relevant.

Yancey, Philip. *Where Is God When It Hurts?* Grand Rapids, Mich.: Zondervan Publishing House, 1977. Winner of the Gold Medallion Award for Excellence in Christian Publishing, this book is probably the best single volume on pain and suffering.

ACKNOWLEDGMENT

Insight for Living gratefully acknowledges permission from the
Saint Andrew Press, Edinburgh, Scotland, for generous use of the
excellent source noted below.

Barclay, William. *The Letters of James and Peter,* rev. ed., The Daily
Study Bible series. Philadelphia, Pa.: Westminster Press, 1976.

ORDERING INFORMATION

Cassette Tapes and Study Guide

This Bible study guide was designed to be used independently or in conjunction with the broadcast of Chuck Swindoll's taped messages on the topic listed below. If you would like to order cassette tapes or further copies of this study guide, please see the information given below and the Order Form provided on the last page of this guide.

JAMES . . . PRACTICAL AND AUTHENTIC LIVING

As you study these messages, you'll be convinced James has been looking through your keyhole. With penetrating force, each section of James talks about how to live for God in an authentic way that is altogether unique and rare. This book of the Bible really gets down to the practical way you live. It answers the question, "If you say you believe like you should, then why do you behave like you shouldn't?" James helps you get off the fence and move in a direction that could ultimately change your life.

			Calif.*	U.S.	B.C.*	Canada*
JAM	SG	Study Guide	$ 6.31	$ 5.95	$ 7.64	$ 7.64
JAM	CS	Cassette series, includes album cover	69.17	65.25	93.79	88.81
JAM	1–12	Individual cassettes, include messages A and B	5.30	5.00	7.18	6.79

*These prices already include the following charges: for delivery in **California,** 6% sales tax; **Canada,** 7% postage and handling; **British Columbia,** 6% British Columbia sales tax (on tapes only) and 7% postage and handling. The prices are subject to change without notice.

JAM   1A: *A Case for Practical Christianity*—Survey of James
         B: *Marks of a Practical Christian*—Psalm 15

JAM   2A: *When Troubles Won't Go Away*—James 1: 2–12
         B: *How to Trust When You're Troubled*—Job 1–2:10

JAM   3A: *Plain Talk about Temptation*—James 1:13–18
         B: *How to Say No When Lust Says Yes*—Genesis 39

How to Order by Mail

Simply mark on the order form whether you want the series or individual tapes. Mail the form with your payment to the appropriate address listed below. We will process your order as promptly as we can.

United States: Mail your order to the Sales Department at Insight for Living, Post Office Box 4444, Fullerton, California 92634. If you wish your order to be shipped first-class for faster delivery, add 10 percent of the total order amount. Otherwise, please allow four to six weeks for delivery by fourth-class mail. We accept personal checks, money orders, Visa, or MasterCard in payment for materials. Unfortunately, we are unable to offer invoicing or COD orders.

Canada: Mail your order to Insight for Living Ministries, Post Office Box 2510, Vancouver, British Columbia V6B 3W7. Allow approximately four weeks for delivery. We accept personal checks, money orders, Visa, or MasterCard in payment for materials. Unfortunately, we are unable to offer invoicing or COD orders.

Australia, New Zealand, or Papua New Guinea: Mail your order to Insight for Living, Inc., GPO Box 2823 EE, Melbourne, Victoria 3001, Australia. Please allow six to ten weeks for delivery by surface mail. If you would like your order sent airmail, the delivery time may be reduced. Using the United States price as a base, add postage costs—surface or airmail—to the amount of your order. Please use the chart that follows to determine correct postage. Due to fluctuating currency rates, we can accept only personal checks made payable in U.S. funds, international money orders, Visa, or MasterCard in payment for materials.

Overseas: Other overseas residents should mail their orders to our United States office. Please allow six to ten weeks for delivery by surface mail. If you would like your order sent airmail, the delivery time may be reduced. Using the United States price as a base, add postage costs—surface or airmail—to the amount of your order. Please use the chart that follows to determine correct postage. Due to fluctuating currency rates, we can accept only personal checks made payable in U.S. funds, international money orders, Visa, or MasterCard in payment for materials.

Type of Postage	Postage Cost
Surface	10% of total order
Airmail	25% of total order

For Faster Service, Order by Telephone or FAX

For Visa or MasterCard orders, you are welcome to use one of our toll-free numbers between the hours of 8:00 A.M. and 4:30 P.M., Pacific time, Monday through Friday, or our FAX numbers. The numbers to use from anywhere in the United States are **1-800-772-8888** or FAX (714) 773-0932. To order from Canada, call our Vancouver office using **1-800-663-7639** or FAX (604) 596-2975. Vancouver residents, call (604) 596-2910. Australian residents should phone (03) 872-4606. From overseas, call our Sales Department at (714) 870-9161 in the United States.

Our Guarantee

Our cassettes are guaranteed for ninety days against faulty performance or breakage due to a defect in the tape. For best results, please be sure your tape recorder is in good operating condition and is cleaned regularly.

Note: To cover processing and handling, there is a $10 fee for *any* returned check.

Order Form

JAM CS represents the entire *James . . . Practical and Authentic Living* series in a special album cover, while JAM 1–12 are the individual tapes included in the series. JAM SG represents this study guide, should you desire to order additional copies.

Item	Calif.*	U.S.	B.C.*	Canada*	Quantity	Amount
		Unit Price				
JAM CS	$69.17	$65.25	$93.79	$88.81		$
JAM 1	5.30	5.00	7.18	6.79		
JAM 2	5.30	5.00	7.18	6.79		
JAM 3	5.30	5.00	7.18	6.79		
JAM 4	5.30	5.00	7.18	6.79		
JAM 5	5.30	5.00	7.18	6.79		
JAM 6	5.30	5.00	7.18	6.79		
JAM 7	5.30	5.00	7.18	6.79		
JAM 8	5.30	5.00	7.18	6.79		
JAM 9	5.30	5.00	7.18	6.79		
JAM 10	5.30	5.00	7.18	6.79		
JAM 11	5.30	5.00	7.18	6.79		
JAM 12	5.30	5.00	7.18	6.79		
JAM SG	6.31	5.95	7.64	7.64		
					Subtotal	
		Overseas Residents Pay U.S. price plus 10% surface postage or 25% airmail. Also, see "How to Order by Mail."				
		U.S. First-Class Shipping For faster delivery, add 10% for postage and handling.				
		Gift to Insight for Living Tax-deductible in the United States and Canada.				
		Total Amount Due Please do not send cash.				$

If there is a balance: ☐ apply it as a donation   ☐ please refund
*These prices already include applicable taxes and shipping costs.

Payment by: ☐ Check or money order made payable to Insight for Living or

☐ Credit card (circle one):   Visa   MasterCard   Number _____

   Expiration Date _____   Signature _____
   We cannot process your credit card purchase without your signature.

Name _____

Address _____

City _____   State/Province _____

Zip/Postal Code _____   Country _____

Telephone (____) _____   Radio Station ___ ___ ___ ___
If questions arise concerning your order, we may need to contact you.

Mail this order form to the Sales Department at one of these addresses:
Insight for Living, Post Office Box 4444, Fullerton, CA 92634
Insight for Living Ministries, Post Office Box 2510, Vancouver, BC, Canada V6B 3W7
Insight for Living, Inc., GPO Box 2823 EE, Melbourne, VIC 3001, Australia

Broadcast Schedule

James . . . Practical and Authentic Living
April 18–June 24, 1991

Thursday	April 18	**A Case for Practical Christianity**
		Survey of James
Friday	April 19	**A Case for Practical Christianity**

Monday	April 22	**Marks of a Practical Christian**
		Psalm 15
Tuesday	April 23	**Marks of a Practical Christian**
Wednesday	April 24	**When Troubles Won't Go Away**
		James 1: 2–12
Thursday	April 25	**When Troubles Won't Go Away**
Friday	April 26	**How to Trust When You're Troubled**
		Job 1–2:10

Monday	April 29	**How to Trust When You're Troubled**
Tuesday	April 30	**Plain Talk about Temptation**
		James 1:13–18
Wednesday	May 1	**Plain Talk about Temptation**
Thursday	May 2	**How to Say No When Lust Says Yes**
		Genesis 39
Friday	May 3	**How to Say No When Lust Says Yes**

Monday	May 6	**The Great Divorce**
		James 1:19–27
Tuesday	May 7	**The Great Divorce**
Wednesday	May 8	**Prescription for Marriage on the Rocks**
		Psalm 51
Thursday	May 9	**Prescription for Marriage on the Rocks**
Friday	May 10	**Prejudice Is a Sin**
		James 2:1–13

Monday	May 13	**Prejudice Is a Sin**
Tuesday	May 14	**How to Discern without Judging**
		1 Samuel 16:1–13
Wednesday	May 15	**How to Discern without Judging**
Thursday	May 16	**You Can't Have One without the Other**
		James 2:14–26
Friday	May 17	**You Can't Have One without the Other**

Monday	May 20	**Justified by Works**
		Genesis 22:1–14
Tuesday	May 21	**Justified by Works**
Wednesday	May 22	**Bridling the Beast in Your Body**
		James 3:1–12
Thursday	May 23	**Bridling the Beast in Your Body**
Friday	May 24	**How to Muzzle Your Mouth**
		Psalm 39

Monday	May 27	**How to Muzzle Your Mouth**
Tuesday	May 28	**The Wise, the Unwise, and the Otherwise (Part One)**
		James 3:13–16
Wednesday	May 29	**The Wise, the Unwise, and the Otherwise (Part One)**
Thursday	May 30	**The Wise, the Unwise, and the Otherwise (Part Two)**
		James 3:13, 17–18
Friday	May 31	**The Wise, the Unwise, and the Otherwise (Part Two)**

Monday	June 3	**How Fights Are Started and Stopped**
		James 4:1–10
Tuesday	June 4	**How Fights Are Started and Stopped**
Wednesday	June 5	**When Is It Right to Fight?**
		Selected Scripture
Thursday	June 6	**When Is It Right to Fight?**
Friday	June 7	**The Peril of Playing God**
		James 4:11–17

Monday	June 10	**The Peril of Playing God**
Tuesday	June 11	**Warnings to the Wealthy**
		James 5:1–6
Wednesday	June 12	**Warnings to the Wealthy**
Thursday	June 13	**Doing Right When You've Been Done Wrong**
		James 5:7–12
Friday	June 14	**Doing Right When You've Been Done Wrong**

Monday	June 17	**Suffering, Sickness, Sin—and Healing**
		James 5:13–16
Tuesday	June 18	**Suffering, Sickness, Sin—and Healing**
Wednesday	June 19	**The Power of Effective Kneeling**
		James 5:13–18
Thursday	June 20	**The Power of Effective Kneeling**
Friday	June 21	**How to Handle Straying Saints**
		James 5:19–20

Monday	June 24	**How to Handle Straying Saints**

Insight for Living • Post Office Box 4444, Fullerton, CA 92634
Insight for Living Ministries • Post Office Box 2510, Vancouver, BC, Canada V6B 3W7
Insight for Living, Inc. • GPO Box 2823 EE, Melbourne, VIC 3001, Australia

ORDER FORM

This special book offer expires July 31, 1991.

Title	California*	U.S.	Canada*	Quantity	Amount
Kingdoms in Conflict (softcover)	$10.55	$9.95	$12.78	_____	$ _____
James: Bible Study Commentary (softcover)	7.37	6.95	8.92	_____	_____
Honesty, Morality, and Conscience (softcover)	9.49	8.95	11.49	_____	_____

Subtotal $ _____

For faster shipping, United States residents can add 10 percent for first-class shipping and handling _____

Contribution to the Insight for Living radio ministry _____
All contributions are tax-deductible.

Total Amount Enclosed $ _____
Check or money order should be made payable to Insight for Living.

* Prices include applicable taxes and shipping costs.

Credit card purchases:

☐ Visa   ☐ MasterCard Number _____

Expiration Date _____

Signature _____
We cannot process your credit card purchase without your signature.

For Visa and MasterCard orders, you are welcome to use one of our toll-free numbers between the hours of 8:00 A.M. and 4:30 P.M., Pacific time, Monday through Friday, or our FAX numbers. The numbers to use from anywhere in the United States are **1-800-772-8888** or FAX (714) 773-0932. To order from Canada, call our Vancouver office using **1-800-663-7639** or FAX (604) 596-2975. Vancouver residents, call (604) 596-2910.

Name _____

Address _____

City _____

State/Province _____ Zip/Postal Code _____

Country _____

Telephone ( ) _____ Radio Station __ __ __ __
If questions arise concerning your order, we may need to contact you.

Insight for Living • Post Office Box 4444, Fullerton, CA 92634
Insight for Living Ministries • Post Office Box 2510, Vancouver, BC, Canada V6B 3W7

Please allow four to six weeks for delivery.

INSIGHT FOR LIVING

JAMES . . . PRACTICAL AND AUTHENTIC LIVING

SPECIAL BOOK OFFER

The book of James presents authentic and godly living that is practical, unique, and rare. Each section will impact your life with penetrating force. You'll be challenged to get off the fence and live your life as an exciting adventure. We'd like to offer you these excellent books which, we feel certain, will enhance your studies in this provocative epistle.

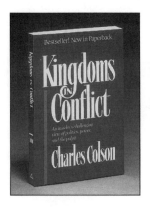

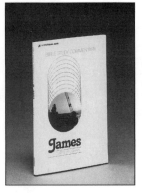

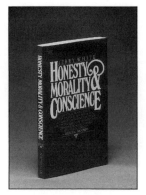

Kingdoms in Conflict

This stimulating volume will encourage you to exhibit your faith through works of social action. Topics include the conflict between church and state, the role of Christians in politics, and civil disobedience. Author Charles Colson sends a sober message expounding the dangers of either politicized or privatized faith.

James: Bible Study Commentary

Written by Curtis Vaughan and formerly titled *James: A Study Guide,* this important expositional and devotional commentary acts as an instructor for anyone who seeks to understand the truth of James. Vaughan includes illuminating translations of pertinent Greek words and phrases as a basis for insight and application.

Honesty, Morality, and Conscience

Living ethically is tough. Jerry White provides us realistic guidelines and workable answers to our moral dilemmas. He explores questionable business practices, declining morals, superficial relationships, and self-deceit—all of which cause ethical confusion. Excellent for all who seek to exhibit salt and light in an increasingly decadent society.